What struck me immediately about this book was the author's deep love and care for the people of Burma, as well as the close relationships he built to earn their trust. My family has been serving in Burma for over thirty-one years, and we have been both inspired and educated by this book. The nuances of life, the importance of religion, tribe, culture, and social standing ground this work in the truths of Burma. At the same time, the supernatural intervention of Jesus shines clearly.

Read this book to be inspired, to gain knowledge, to discover new perspectives, and for the joy of learning about new people and how they met Jesus. *Jesus in the Buddha Belt* encourages me to lift my eyes to heaven in gratitude and love, and to approach others with openness and compassion. It strengthens my faith and reinforces my belief that we serve a faithful, loving, and supernaturally powerful God who has the answers to all our problems. I thank God for Ben and his family, for how they have lived and for sharing their experiences with Jesus and the people of Burma.

DAVID EUBANK
Founder, Free Burma Rangers

Jesus in the Buddha Belt introduces four previously inaccessible biographies from a little-known part of the world. I love that it shows off God's power without hiding human weakness. It is uplifting, enlightening, and entertaining—a great new resource for anyone wanting to learn how to better pray for mission to Buddhists, for those going on short-term mission trips, and for those preparing or serving in long-term mission to Buddhists.

JOHANNES BAUER
Field Operations Director, YWAM (Myanmar)

"Example often speaks louder than precept." That adage is certainly proven true in *Jesus in the Buddha Belt*. Ben Wilder possesses a powerful gift for combining both precept and example as he shares true accounts of Christ's transforming power in the deceptive environment of Buddhism.

TOM ELLIFF, DMin
Former President, International Mission Board

In *Jesus in the Buddha Belt*, Ben helps us rethink the image of Jesus that many people in Myanmar have grown up with. He talks about how colonial powers, like the British and Americans, not only brought their religion but also left behind a lasting image of Jesus that was tied to oppression rather than freedom. By sharing personal stories and reflections, the author encourages us to see Jesus in a way that feels more real and connected to the people of Myanmar—one that strips away the colonial baggage and focuses on Jesus's true Middle Eastern roots. The book highlights how important it is to be sensitive to different cultures and to represent Jesus in a way that respects local traditions and identities. It's a powerful reminder that how we see Jesus can be shaped by history, and that we need to work toward a version of Jesus that speaks meaningfully to people everywhere.

Jon Foltz
Director of Leadership Development, Thailand Campus Crusade, CRU

Ben Wilder takes us into the heart of Buddhism for a deeply authentic experience with former Buddhists who have encountered true enlightenment through Jesus and have had their worlds turned upside down and transformed by God's love. History is being made right now in the Buddhist world. Come have your eyes opened to both the incredible challenges and the mind-blowing miracles of God's work in this final frontier of missions, the Buddhist Belt. My family has been serving Jesus in the Buddhist world for over fifteen years, and this book was still deeply insightful and inspiring for me. I know it will be for you too! Pull up a chair and find a hot cup of milk tea for a window into a world you might not know anything about, but as a follower of Jesus, you are being invited to engage.

John Hogan
Leader, Golden Shores Initiative

Jesus in the Buddha Belt drew me into a world both truly foreign and equally familiar. While I have served in church planting and missions for over thirty-five years, Aung, Bawi, Lin, and Tha Gyi guided me to a new place. They took me to the country of Myanmar and exposed me to the diverse geography, history, culture, peoples, and religions of this foreign place. But on the familiar side, these four share their stories with a humanity and vulnerability that's New Testament-like. They share fear and doubt, failure, and persecution, but also courage, faithfulness, victory, and spiritual fruit. Through all of this, they pointed me to God and the saving grace of Jesus Christ for all the world. Their stories challenged and encouraged me and reminded me again of the Great Commission to make disciples of all peoples.

Adam Johnson
Emeritus Missionary, IMB
Digital Evangelism Coach, Kavanah Media

Myanmar is a contested nation ravaged by conflicts, a fertile ground for the Gospel, a sleeping giant awaiting glorious awakening and transformation. The stories of Myanmar's inspirational and courageous missions must be told. In this book, Ben will take you up close to these stories as one who labored among them, not merely as an armchair missiologist, including costly lessons learned with many tears and joy. Reading this book brings us to a deeper appreciation of the Spirit inscribed in Hebrews 11:38–40. This book is a must for everyone who cares about finishing Jesus's Great Commission!

DANIEL LIM
Global Intercession Leader

Having walked alongside Ben in some of the very villages and cities brought to life in *Jesus in the Buddha Belt*, I can attest to the depth of faith, love, and authenticity that runs throughout this book. These stories vividly capture the heartbeat of Myanmar and provide profound cultural and spiritual insights into the lives of its people and the unique challenges they face. The author's deep love for Myanmar and his ability to weave their struggles and triumphs into compelling first-person narratives will stir your heart and renew your passion for God's mission. Whether you're a seasoned missionary or simply curious about the beauty of Christ's work in a Buddhist context, this book not only offers an inspiring and deeply personal glimpse into God's redemptive power in the most unexpected places but also an invitation to join him in the work.

GREG MANN, MDiv
Affinity Group Leader for the Asia-Pacific Rim Peoples Affinity, IMB

Insightful, descriptive, wise, and rich! Ben has tapped his years of experience in Myanmar to bring us a book that deals with its myriads of contexts in a readable and informative way. Ben uses the stories to skillfully and sensitively share about Buddhism, how God is at work, and to highlight some failures that might make you wince. If you read this book, I believe you will come away better informed and encouraged to pray. I have long respected Ben and his family. To me, they display authenticity in their passion for the gospel, as well as their calling and commitment to the people of Myanmar.

HUGH MARTIN
Field Leader in Myanmar, OMF

Ben Wilder shares compelling and convicting stories of the lives and experiences of people who are very different in religion, customs, and culture from those in the West. The book teaches the hope of Jesus's saving and transforming grace in the modern Buddhist world. Wilder shows how disciples of Jesus can understand a Buddhist way of thinking and culture as they come to understand the truth of Jesus and learn to love others above their own culture, biases, and perspectives.

ISRAEL MARTINEZ, MDiv
Acts 29 Network Church Planter
Lead Pastor, Redeemer Church, Irving, TX

With over twenty years of experience living and working in Myanmar (Burma), the author brings tremendous depth of understanding to a calling and task that requires mature spiritual inspiration. I hope you sense that the author is thrilled by his calling, even amid chaotic and often dangerous circumstances. This book offers a rare qualitative look into three Southeast Asian tribes, providing a personal, on-the-ground perspective often missing in data-driven religious studies. Aung, Bawi, Lin, and Tha Gyi provide a compelling account of why they found conversion to Christ difficult and the supernatural power of God to overcome the obstacles to faith in a Buddhist context.

If you are reading it in a study group, the interaction sections will help the group digest the experiences of the main characters. Some may wonder how the stories of four individuals in one country can represent the experience "in the Buddha Belt" that stretches across Southeast Asia. However, if you read it with a Vietnamese, Cambodian, or Thai group, you'll see them light up with recognition of realities they have also experienced.

MICHAEL POCOCK, DMiss
Department Chair Emeritus and Senior Professor Emeritus of
Missiology & Intercultural Ministries, Dallas Theological Seminary

In *Jesus in the Buddha Belt*, Wilder ingeniously employs the oft-neglected vehicle of storytelling for spiritual formation and missiological wisdom. Through the stories of four diverse people from war-torn Myanmar, we encounter the daunting challenges to faithful and flourishing witness to Jesus in this land. Yet alongside the heartbreaking failures and pitfalls to be avoided are inspiring testimonies of gospel breakthroughs that point to promising ways forward for Jesus-followers. In this way, Wilder uncovers the entrenched historical, cultural, and religious barriers to the gospel in the Buddha Belt while also instilling hope in the goodness and power of Jesus to overcome any barrier. The lessons learned through these stories shed light on how we might best experience sustainable growth of the kingdom of God, not only in Myanmar and Theravada Buddhist contexts, but in other least-reached environments throughout the world. The author has enhanced the usefulness and transformative potential of his book through thoughtful reflection questions and abundant resources for prayer and action. All in all, this book delivers a goldmine of wisdom in a compelling and captivating way.

TODD POKRIFKA, PhD
Co-Director of the Institute for Community Transformation,
Frontier Ventures

A book about missions should accomplish three key things: first, it should provide a clear sense of the country where the work is taking place—in this case, Myanmar. Second, it should inspire a deep love and compassion for the people. Finally, it should leave readers questioning whether they, too, are called to go. As we read, we should ask God if he is calling us. *Jesus in the Buddha Belt* hits all three in a surprising way. Reading people's stories in the first person gives the reader a sense of the culture and why it is so difficult for them to come to faith. These stories also provide an honest sense of why reaching them is so challenging and, at the same time, convey the urgency of going. I've known Ben for many years. He loves Jesus deeply and believes in his call to the nations. Read with empathy and an openness to God's call on your life. I highly recommend this book.

STEVEN SMITH, PhD
Former Associate Dean and Assistant Professor,
Southwestern Baptist Theological Seminary
Author, *Dying to Preach: Embracing the Cross in the Pulpit*

Ben masterfully crafts compelling stories that bring to light the complexities of missions in Myanmar. He does so with deep insight and heartfelt empathy that can only come from real experience tempered by a heart of love. It is such a delight to get immersed in the experiences of the characters as they tell their captivating stories. The hard truth is that missions is messy, but God somehow still transforms the lives of people through it all. I was uplifted by this book as I encountered God in these true stories.

SONG TJOA, DMin, MBA
Senior Minister, New Life Fellowship of Churches
Founder, Clarion Newlife Capital

This book has had a profound impact on me, revealing at least two powerful truths. First, God used it to teach me about a culture and a people I knew little about, showing me the incredible ways He is working in their lives. Second, it reminded me that God operates in powerful, life-changing ways that go beyond what we can see. I was deeply challenged to live a life of intentional faith, walking by trust and not by sight. The real-life stories shared in this book are both humbling and inspiring—stories of how God is reaching everyday people, transforming their lives, and calling them to serve.

The author does a remarkable job of telling these testimonies, painting vivid pictures of his friends' journeys and drawing me into their lives. Though some parts of the stories are difficult to read—addressing real struggles and the hardships that come with following Jesus—the honesty and authenticity are refreshing. The book ends with a powerful challenge: What will I do in response to these stories?

If you're looking for a book that will open your eyes to the global work of God, challenge your faith, and inspire you to take bold steps in your own walk with him, this is a must-read.

GAYLORD TSUEI (崔磊), MDiv
Caring Pastor, Austin Chinese Church

Having twenty years of personal experience and research in Southeast Asia, the author is a dedicated Christian missionary with a passion for evangelizing the Burmese, and his remarkable storytelling ability brings readers into the heart of his journey. Through his writing, I've had the privilege of meeting Aung, Bawi, Lin, and Gyi, and witnessing their profound spiritual transformations. Ben's work shines a light on the incredible impact God is having in the Buddha Belt. Furthermore, he inspires Christians to engage in meaningful dialogue between Buddhist beliefs and Christian faith, fostering a deeper understanding of cultures, religions, and histories. His captivating writing style prepares us to pray for and share the gospel with others more effectively.

I am deeply moved and amazed! Not only is Ben gifted in writing, but he is also a great narrator, able to completely bring readers into the life stories he describes, making them feel like they are there and experiencing the same emotions. I firmly believe that this book will provide many valuable experiences and inspirations to Christians who are interested in evangelizing among Buddhist groups!

REV. LUKE ZHANG (張路加 牧師), DMin
Director of Chinese Ministry, The Sowers International
Founder and Missionary, Europe Campus Ministry
President, The Hidden Manna Media Mission International

Jesus
IN THE
BUDDHA
BELT

Untold True Stories
of a Mighty God
and Messy Mission

BEN WILDER

visit us at missionbooks.org

Jesus in the Buddha Belt: Untold True Stories of a Mighty God and Messy Mission

© 2025 by Ben Wilder. All Rights Reserved.

No part of this book may be reproduced, stored in a retrieval system, or transmitted in any form or by any means—electronic, mechanical, photocopy, recording, or otherwise—without prior written permission from the publisher, except brief quotations used in connection with reviews.

This manuscript may not be entered into AI, even for AI training.
For permission, email permissions@wclbooks.com.
For corrections, email editor@wclbooks.com.

William Carey Publishing (WCP) publishes resources to shape and advance the missiological conversation in the world. We publish a broad range of thought-provoking books and do not necessarily endorse all opinions set forth here or in works referenced within this book.

The URLs included in this book are provided for personal use only and are current as of the date of publication, but the publisher disclaims any obligation to update them after publication.

Scripture quotations are taken from the Christian Standard Bible®, Copyright © 2017 by Holman Bible Publishers. Used by permission. Christian Standard Bible® and CSB® are federally registered trademarks of Holman Bible Publishers.

Published by William Carey Publishing
10 W. Dry Creek Cir
Littleton, CO 80120 | www.missionbooks.org

William Carey Publishing is a ministry of Frontier Ventures
Pasadena, CA | www.frontierventures.org

Front Cover Designer: Ben Wilder
Back Cover and Interior Designer: Mike Riester
Illustrations by Hnin Nadi Aung (hninnadi.hna@gmail.com)

ISBNs: 978-1-64508-645-1 (paperback)
       978-1-64508-647-5 (epub)

Printed Worldwide

29 28 27 26 25   1 2 3 4 5   IN

Library of Congress Control Number: 2025934426

I dedicate this book
with deep gratitude to:

Dad, for making me a craftsman.
Mom, for nursing me in selfless grace.
My bride, for holding my hand on the road less traveled.
Nebs, whatcha gonna do when you go to college?

Yahweh, for art, love, and one-upping karma.
And you, for picking up this book.
I can't thank each one
of you enough.

> "What comes into our minds when we think about God is the most important thing about us."
>
> —A. W. Tozer

Contents

Author's Promise and Invitation	xiii
Welcome to the Buddha Belt	xvii

PART 1 AUNG'S STORY
A Buddhist Monk's Life Takes a Supernatural Turn

Unexpected Answer	3
Divorce or Miracle?	13
Thant and the Crazy Christians	23
Going Deeper: Trail Guides to Jesus	31

PART 2 BAWI'S STORY
Conversion from Christian Tradition to The Real Jesus

Awakening	45
Village Fire	53
Love and Blindfolds	63
Going Deeper: Becoming Like a Buddhist (to Win Some to Jesus)	73

PART 3 LIN'S STORY
The Bright and Dark Side of Christian Mission in Myanmar

Adoption	85
Murder Plot	95
Inside Addiction	105
Going Deeper: A Prince, the Bride, and Jesus	117

PART 4 THA GYI'S STORY
Unprecedented Opportunity in the Urban Youth Scene

Yangon City Lights	129
New Friends, New Life	139
Something Missing	145
Going Deeper: Repainting the White Colonialist Jesus	153
Epilogue: Our New Friends Now and Where We Go From Here	161
Appendix 1: Discussion and Prayer Guide	165
Appendix 2: Insights for Mission	175
Appendix 3: How to Use Jesusinthebuddhabelt.com	183
Suggestions for Further Reading	185
Acknowledgments	187

Author's Promise and Invitation

Here we are. This is a big moment. I have spent over twenty years researching and hundreds of hours preparing this book for you. And you, through a series of causes and events unknown to me, are now holding it in your hands, contemplating. Thank you.

Right now, you are probably considering the risks and rewards of the three to four hours you might spend reading this book. *Will it be worth it?* I want to help answer that question.

But first, let's introduce ourselves. I'm Ben. I'd like to know a little about you. I'm guessing you might be one of three people.

1. If you are a Christian looking for compelling biographies to expand your view of God and inspire your personal faith journey, welcome. I think you will find help here. The stories in this book have certainly done that for me.

2. If you are interested in mission to Buddhists (at home or abroad) as a prayer supporter, short- or long-term missionary, a sending or training organization, or someone who wants to share the gospel with your Buddhist neighbors or coworkers, welcome. I hope you find the narrative form of this book a refreshing and helpful supplement to the typical academic approach in this sphere. You might find this book useful as a training manual in disguise.

3. If you are a Buddhist who's interested in Jesus, or someone who grew up Christian who's interested in Buddhism, welcome. I can relate. Please keep reading and I think you will find help here too.

Whichever of these wonderful people you are, nice to meet you. I have written this book for you. Here's what I think you might gain from reading it, in the form of a personal story.

Wide-eyed and open-hearted, I traveled from the Bible Belt to the Buddha Belt over twenty years ago with a thousand thoughts and feelings about Jesus, Buddha, and the seemingly backward people of Myanmar. What I discovered was very different from what I expected, but exactly what my hungry heart needed. Why? Because A. W. Tozer was right in *The Knowledge of the Holy*: "What comes into our minds when we think about God is the most important thing about us."

The simple people of faith that I sat and drank tea with, in the Buddha Belt changed what comes into my mind when I think of God. Why? Because Jesus was right: "Blessed are you who are poor, because the kingdom of God is yours ... But woe to you who are rich, for you have received your comfort" (Luke 6:20b, 24).

In many ways, the inspiring people I met in the Buddha Belt had less than I did. They were materially poor, and their lives were difficult; we might think them disadvantaged. But in other ways, they had substantially more than me—they were spiritually rich because of their deep connection to God. That sent me back to the drawing board. I had been a Christian for years, heard thousands of sermons, and spent endless hours studying the Bible. But I had to admit that these poor people, with much less Bible knowledge, were more desperate for God and experiencing him in a deeper way than I was. I'm not trying to minimize Bible knowledge, and I'm not trying to put these people on a pedestal; you will soon find out they're as imperfect as you and me. Still, I could not deny the truth—they had a deeper faith and experience of God than I did.

Sitting in the Buddha Belt with the materially poor—yet spiritually rich—everyday heroes of the faith, with all their imperfections, expanded my view of God and beckoned me to join them in a deeper experience of Jesus. They also taught me a lot about God's mission and how to reach Buddhists for Jesus—even with my imperfections.

I think meeting these simple saints would challenge and bless you too. But you probably can't get on a plane to the Buddha Belt right now. Even if you could, you probably don't have years to invest learning a new language, a foreign culture, and building deep relationships. But I bet you can join me for a few more pages. Here's my promise if you do:

- In the following pages, you will gain four new friends from the Buddha Belt—real people whose lives have been radically changed by God—and learn from their epic failures as well as their smashing successes.

I expect you will also gain two other benefits from reading this book if you approach it with a hungry heart and an open mind, but you'll have to work this part out between God and you.

- The new friends you meet in this book might change your life. As I said, they have changed mine—expanding my view of God and deepening my experience of Jesus.
- Finally, this book might inspire and equip you to be used by God in changing the lives of others (either at home or abroad).

Will this book be worth it for you? I only know one way to find out. Will you pull up a chair and take this journey with me?

This is my personal invitation to you.

—Ben Wilder

CLAIM YOUR FREE GIFT BUNDLE NOW

jesusinthebuddhabelt.com/gift

Thank you so much for picking up this book! It wouldn't exist without you! Scan the QR code or enter the URL above to download a free gift bundle, including an exclusive bonus chapter and a high-resolution prayer map of the Buddha Belt.

Welcome to the Buddha Belt

At different times in the not-so-distant past, Abraham Lincoln and Adolf Hitler were both unimportant names. But when each man's moment came, he rose from the shadows of obscurity to leave an indelible mark on our history—one for good and one for evil. At the present moment, a little-known nation in the heart of Asia's Buddha Belt is in the obscure and unimportant phase: learning, growing, struggling in the fight of its life, waiting for its moment to come—wondering if it ever will—and wondering if the liberating spirit of Lincoln or the heinous spirit of Hitler will prevail.

A SURPRISING GIFT

When I first heard of Myanmar in 2004, I could not even find it on a map. Only after discovering its former name, Burma, did I finally spot its kite-shaped borders sandwiched between India, China, and Thailand. A few months later, with a head full of fanciful ideas, I boarded a plane to see it firsthand. One ocean, four airports, and eleven time zones later, I finally had a bird's-eye view of Myanmar's mystic mountains and valleys scattered with tiny glimmering dots in every direction. Peering through the dirty window at 30,000 feet, I couldn't tell what the spots were. But the confusion cleared as we descended—the tiny, shiny dots were gigantic, gilded pagodas and statues of the Buddha. My heart churned.

The ground below moved faster and faster until the plane bumped to a halt a few minutes later. I slowly stepped off the rolling stairway and planted my feet in Myanmar for the first time. The other passengers scurried off the parking lot-sized runway in a straight line toward the taxi drivers on the other side. I paused to let the moment settle.

Map of the Buddha Belt

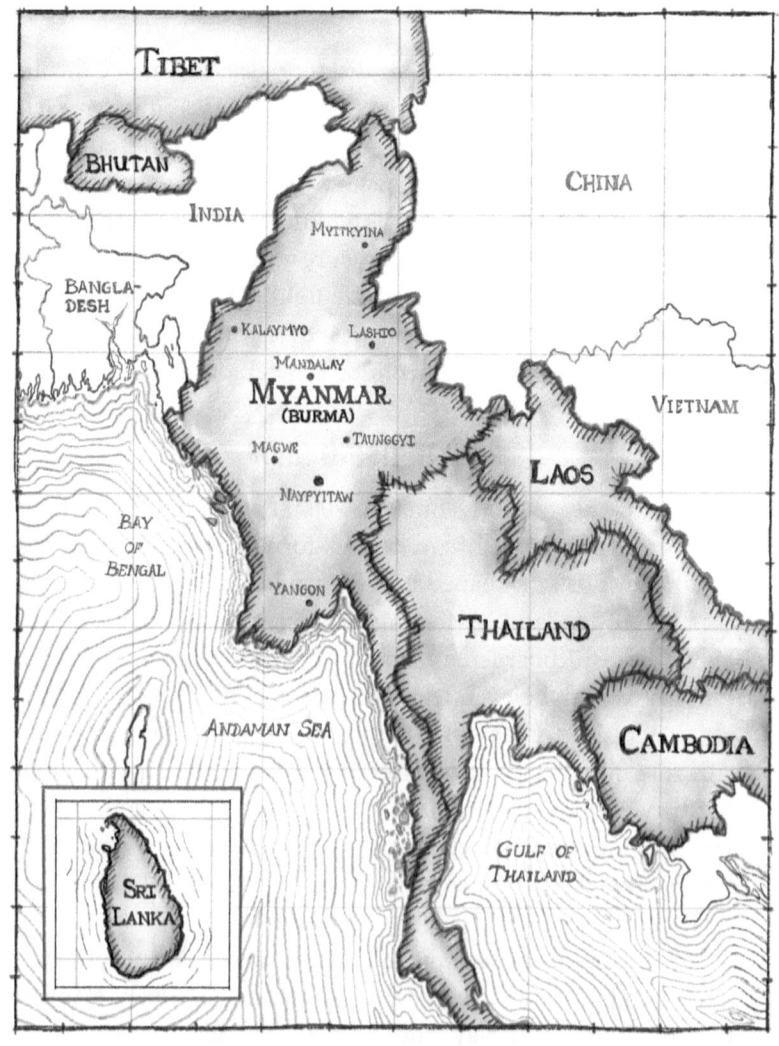

Buddha Belt countries shaded in gray.

My lungs filled to the brim with crisp mountain air, and the last warm rays of the afternoon sun painted my face orange. I still remember my first vivid impression, gazing at the golden-tipped mountains that evening: "God has kissed the earth in this place ... but the people don't know who has done it."

Over two decades later, much of what I originally thought about Myanmar has changed, but that first runway impression has not. The difference now is that I also feel God has kissed *me* in that place—not just with warm sun rays, but with the gift of experiencing Myanmar so deeply, for so many years. I'm writing this book partly to share this gift with you.

In the following pages, you will meet four new friends. I can't wait to introduce them! But before zooming in on the details of their stories, we need a quick, wide-angle view of the place they call home. It is impossible to understand these characters apart from their particular time and place in the Southeast Asian nation of Myanmar. Here is a brief orientation to their tumultuous home.

GLORY TO SHAME

Once considered the top nation in Southeast Asia, Myanmar (formerly Burma) was nearly choked to death by a military stranglehold from 1962 to 2010, when the dictator surprisingly loosened his grip. The nationwide general election in 2011 began a hopeful decade of quasi-democracy and progress led by Nobel Laureate Aung San Suu Kyi's political party, the NLD. Spirits were high after Suu Kyi's party won a landslide victory in the 2020 elections.

It looked as if Myanmar was destined to rise to glory again. But in the early morning darkness of February 1, 2021—the same day the newly elected government planned to hold its first session—the military arrested Aung San Suu Kyi and other key leaders. Minutes later, TVs across the nation announced the military's return to power. A few days after the coup, weaponless citizens bravely took to the streets across the country in unprecedented numbers, peacefully protesting the military takeover and demanding that their votes be respected.

With millions bravely banging pots and waving signs in the face of military oppression, hope rose for a brief moment. Then soldiers and tanks crushed it, firing live rounds at peaceful protesters, bystanders, and anyone else in the way. Thousands of brave dissenters were arrested ... some tortured, some killed, some released, many still missing.

#SAVEMYANMAR

After hope in the political processes, the international community, and ethnic armies all failed, Myanmar freedom fighters fled to the forest for combat training. They returned a few months later with guns and bombs. At the time of this writing, the country has never been embroiled in more chaos; the longing for freedom has never been more acute. Myanmar is dying for change. But is there any real hope that someone might save them?

That is the burning question 58 million Myanmar citizens are pondering from the shadows of obscurity right now, waiting for their moment to come—wondering if it ever will—and wondering if the spirit of Lincoln or Hitler will prevail. Meanwhile, the rest of the Buddha Belt's 180 million inhabitants are embroiled in their own struggles, pondering their own questions, facing their own fears. How will these things resolve? Good or evil, freedom or oppression—which will win the day? Nobody knows. But part of the reason I am writing this book is that I genuinely believe there is hope for a happy ending, and that you and I can cooperate with heaven to affect it.

WHAT IS THE BUDDHA BELT?

I hate to risk messing up a good story with a definition, but I promised you one, so here goes. What is the Buddha Belt? Maybe you have heard the term "Bible Belt" used to describe a region in the Southern United States that is highly influenced by conservative Christianity. On the exact opposite side of the globe, a group of nations in Southeast Asia is similarly dominated by the religion and culture of conservative Buddhism. I am referring to these nations and their 180 million residents as the

Buddha Belt. The Buddha Belt countries—Thailand, Myanmar, Sri Lanka, Cambodia, Laos, Tibet (an autonomous region within China), and Bhutan—are highlighted in the map on page xviii.

Is this book about Myanmar or the Buddha Belt? Yes. The stories in this book take place in Myanmar. And while it's true that each Buddha Belt country has its own particular nuances (please dive into those as needed), these countries also share many broad similarities. So even if it is not a perfect match, I believe much of what we learn in Myanmar will be useful across the region.

FOUR NEW FRIENDS & HOW TO USE THIS BOOK

Let's zoom back into the center of the Buddha Belt, to the wonderful, chaotic country of Myanmar. I'm going to introduce you to four new friends who will tell you about their surprising encounters with Jesus and the gut-wrenching plot twists that follow. A former Buddhist monk, a comfortable Christian, and two urban immigrants—Aung, Bawi, Lin, and Tha Gyi—risk everything to follow Jesus in the midst of war, racial tension, murder plots, betrayal, drug addiction, forbidden love, and the dark side of Christian mission.

I wish you could sit across the table from these friends with a steaming cup of Burmese tea. I wish you could hear the rhythm in their voices, see the emotion in their eyes. Unfortunately, you cannot. But I have written the book in a first-person, spoken style, so it feels like they are sitting across the table, telling their stories to you directly. You will hear from each character for four chapters. The first three chapters tell how they came to know Jesus and everything that has followed. In the fourth chapter, each character steps away from the story and shares their personal view of Jesus and insights into mission. The titles of these chapters begin with "Going Deeper" to indicate the difference.

Note: To protect the four main characters, I've changed their names, omitted specific locations, and avoided using real images. If you recognize them, I ask for your discretion.

At the end of each chapter, I have highlighted one truth about God from the story along with a Scripture. I hope this will help continually draw our focus back to God, even when the story becomes full of human messes. I'm calling these "God Shots," a shameless copy from Tara-Leigh Cobble because her idea was better than all of mine. If you aren't familiar with Tara-Leigh, check out her amazing work at The Bible Recap. After the God Shots, I left space for you to write your own personal reflections.

Tucked away at the back of the book are three little sections to assist those wanting to go further than the body of the text. The first appendix is a "Discussion and Prayer Guide" for each character's story. Use this to facilitate deeper personal reflection, group discussion, and/or prayer. The second appendix, "Insights for Mission," extracts a few mission principles from each chapter's story in a concise summary form. The third appendix is an index of a few key terms and topics to aid in sharing the gospel with Buddhists. Students and teachers of mission will find these helpful for reference, retention, and conversation.

Our team has also built jesusinthebuddhabelt.com to facilitate ongoing learning, conversation, and mission opportunities. We hope you find it a helpful way to dig deeper, stay connected, and share with friends. I invite you to explore the website right now and sign up to get free ongoing updates and resources from our team. And let us know your thoughts on how to make it better.

In the meantime, I hope you enjoy getting to know these new friends. I hope they show you God and the other side of the world in compelling and possibly new ways. I also hope they increase your understanding of people different from you, so you can better love, pray for, and communicate the gospel to them—whether they are Buddhists across the world or next-door neighbors. Okay, enough hoping. Are you ready to meet Aung?

Part 1
Aung's Story

A BUDDHIST MONK'S LIFE TAKES A SUPERNATURAL TURN

Aung contemplating life as a Buddhist monk

1
Unexpected Answer

He pressed the tip of the cold black barrel against my clammy forehead. "Do it, fool. Or else." I swallowed hard, leaned against the plaster wall, and looked to the stars for courage. I would be shamed and beaten if caught. But chickening out would be even worse. I slowly reached up to the rough wooden windowsill. It was open. My sideways head craned just high enough to peer inside with one eye. There he was, still sleeping. *Get yourself together, Aung. Nothing bad is going to happen.* I gathered my nerve, inched to my feet, and climbed through the window in slow motion. Halfway across the room toward the stack of cookie tins—bang! My fellow novice monk stood up, fired the toy gun, and dashed away. The elder monk startled and rolled over. *"Ama-lay Paya!"* I whisper-cursed and bounded out the window, scared-dog style.

A few nerve-racking seconds later, my trigger-happy colleague shook with silent laughter under the blanket next to me. The other novices were already in deep, rhythmic sleep. I tried to slow my breath to match theirs. But I couldn't. My heart was racing. My mind was racing. And my lungs were still trying to catch up. Would an angry senior monk burst through the door any moment? Or had he even woken up? Why on earth did I do that? These were the first deep questions I pondered growing up in the Buddhist monastery. Okay, maybe the actual deep questions came later, but these sure felt deep to a ten-year-old boy who had just attempted midnight cookie theft. All that, and I didn't even get to enjoy a cookie.

A LONG DIRT TRAIL

My parents called me Aung at birth. That's the name I've gone by all my life, except for the years I wore a monk's robe. My tiny mountain village is farther up a winding dirt trail than you've probably ever wanted to go. It's a trail with no maps, no street signs, no smartphones to show the way; a trail my ancestors blazed with blisters, water buffalo widened with wagons, and Chinese tractors ruined with ruts. Even today, it's only passable on foot in the rainy season—you have to climb it step by step just like my ancestors did. You'll never find it without a guide, and don't bother asking Google. Few human beings even know my people exist, much less where we live. They don't know and don't care—I didn't think anyone did. Then, one day, the most unexpected visitor made it all the way to my cloistered little village in the Buddha Belt. That surprising Jewish carpenter turned everything on its head. He showed me and my belittled people that we matter. He also showed me how to run from an angry mob with sticks. Good thing I already had practice running for attempted cookie theft!

You know why my people wanted to hit me after Jesus visited? I guess it's time to introduce them. Burmese speakers call us Palaung, but we call ourselves Ta'ang. At least a million of us are tucked away in the mountain peaks of Myanmar, China, and Thailand. In many ways, we're no different from you. We scratch out a living, fall in love, and seek a better life for our children. In other ways, we're half a world apart—east and west, rice and bread, poverty and riches, Buddha and Jesus.

I don't know how it is where you live, but family, village, and religion are important to my people. Families live together in small houses with parents, grandparents, and siblings. The family fire burns almost continuously in the middle of the living room, where stories and rules are passed down through generations. Outside our homes—and often *inside* them too—is the village. Each home's front door remains open until dark, turning every village living room into communal property. There's no such thing as privacy, and the group is always more important than the individual.

We have many Ta'ang dialects and traditional clothing variations, but we do not make much of the differences. That would divide us. Most of us cannot name all our Ta'ang subtribes, but we know we are brothers and sisters—all one Ta'ang. That is the message passed down by the elders in every village. Our Ta'ang must stick together. We must work together. We must swim *with* the collective stream of our people—not *against* it. For us, the whole people is more important than any particular village. The whole village is more important than any particular family. And the whole family is more important than any particular individual. We value conformity, not deviation. We have to if we want to survive. But I did the opposite. That's the first thing that got me into trouble after the Jewish carpenter's visit.

My people also value the village. The village knows every generation of your family (past and present), where you go in the morning, and when you come home in the evening. There's no hiding anything—don't even try! And young people's opinions don't mean much. Wisdom comes from the elders. The elders rule the village. And the village tells you what to think. Only fools disagree, which I did. That was the second thing that got me in trouble.

Last but not least, hovering above and woven through every part of my people's family and village fabric, is our traditional religion. Ta'ang people are Buddhist—every one of us. It's not a choice. We're born that way: Ta'ang-Buddhist. You can't change how you're born. That was my third problem, and it got me surrounded by an angry mob with sticks. *Yikes!* But wait, we're not to that part of the story just yet.

CLIMBING THE LADDER

I joined the monastery before my upper lip sprouted hair. I didn't join it from a sense of religious conviction though. True, the monastery is a center of religion, but it also feeds, clothes, and educates young boys for free. My parents weren't the golden umbrella type; they struggled to make ends meet. At the very least, my basic childhood needs would be met at the monastery, and I could choose to leave as an adult if I wanted. On the other hand, if I stuck with it and climbed the ranks, I could become one of the most revered people in society and attain god status.

"Aw-ka-tha, aw-ka-tha, aw-ka-tha ..." Laypeople greet monks by kneeling at their feet, bowing to the ground three times, and chanting this request for protection and forgiveness. The prayer ends by calling the monk *"A-Shin Paya,"* which means god. Laypeople hang on the monk's every word and offer donations as if their present and future lives depend on it—and in their minds, they do. Donations are important for laypeople. It's how they get rid of bad *karma* (sin) and accumulate good *karma* (merit). Since people keep on sinning, they have to keep on giving; that means the monastery keeps on getting. Of course, all monks take a vow of poverty, but it's not easy for higher-level monks to keep this vow since the system never stops pouring money into their alms bowls. This puts many monks in a Judas Iscariot predicament: They are constantly tempted to betray their master for financial gain.

By middle age, after lots of study, practice, and tests, my credentials and reputation made me the top monk in the village. I was as mighty as god and king. The whole village worshipped, revered, and generously donated to me. What more could I ask for? Don't get me wrong, there was a long list of strict rules and regulations to follow—227 plus a few (if you're counting)—but the monk life definitely had its perks. Overall, things were good for me at the top.

Then one day, after a long trip to another town, I rested my tired bones in the living room of a new acquaintance. For a few short minutes, I sat alone while the host went into the kitchen to get refreshments. I'll never forget that fateful moment. My eyes wandered from the pictures on the wall to the furniture, the TV, and, finally, the coffee table. There, right in front of me, sat a small pamphlet written by a fellow Buddhist monk.

HOT HELL

The picture on the front looked interesting, so I grabbed the pamphlet for some casual reading while the host was still out of the room. Before the end of the first page, a life-altering sentence jerked me to a halt: "Hell is hot for a monk who doesn't practice the teaching." I read it again. My mind was racing: 227 rules of monastic behavior, all the junior monks I had taught, the donors who worshipped me. I had vowed to practice the Buddha's teaching—but I couldn't do it. All the while, my worshippers believed I did! The whole thing was a lie! I was headed for hot hell! This truth soaked into me like gasoline: one tiny spark and my whole life would burst into flames.

I left the pamphlet on the table where I found it that day. But the pamphlet didn't leave me. A new inner struggle burned into my conscience that I couldn't shake. I tried to forget it, think about other things, drown it with busyness—nothing worked. The struggle wasn't going away without looking it in the eye. Unfortunately, I couldn't even look myself in the eye. I had to either perfectly practice the Buddha's teaching (which I knew was impossible) or leave the monastery. Those were the only two ways I could think of to be an honest person again. So after lots of hiding, thinking, sweating, and fretting, I did something unthinkable: took off the saffron robe and descended from my mighty throne at the monastery.

Every Buddhist child learns how the Buddha forsook his palace privileges to become a poor hermit and solve the problem of suffering. Every novice monk, including me, reenacts this story as a picture of our own renunciation before putting on the monk robe. Ironically, it now felt like I was reenacting this story for a second time *in reverse*—this time exchanging privilege for poverty as I *left* the golden umbrella of the monastery to reenter normal life. Everybody in the village thought I was a lunatic! Most days I did too! Monks don't step down from god status without some kind of moral failure or major worldly incentive. You better believe the village was buzzing with rumors about the crazy monk who turned in his robe! But let people say what they will; I couldn't live a lie anymore. That was the *hardest* decision of my life—and the *worst* day of my life—until what came next.

After leaving the monastery, I fell in love. Maybe I fell in lust. I don't know. I must admit it was nice returning to the outside world with women after all the cloistered years with monks. Whatever the motive, I married a lady from the village and started a family. That was going okay, except for one of the in-laws. Everybody's got crazy in-laws, but one of my new wife's relatives was too much to take—a backstabber the world would have been better off without. He was Ta'ang. Let me clarify with proper emphasis: He *was* Ta'ang, but he betrayed our people by marrying a Christian Kachin woman and worshipping her foreign god. I put him in his place before he could even open his mouth about that Jesus nonsense. "You're Christian. I am Buddhist. It's better if you don't visit me," I threatened in a roundabout way. And it worked ... for a while.

SHOT IN THE DARK

Then came another day when everything changed. My family was in the financial struggle of our lives, my health was fading, and I couldn't do anything about it. Finally, at my wit's end, I told my wife to take the kids to her parents' house and find a job. I was going to stay home and do the only thing I could—rest and hope for a miracle. That night as I lay alone in the little bamboo hut, the illness grabbed me and dragged me to the edge of death.

I knew I would never see the sun rise again. Then, I suddenly heard the strangest sound. It was a voice I had heard before—but never let into my ears. It was so loud now that I couldn't hear anything else; I had to pay attention. The voice said three solitary words: "Jesus is Savior." To be honest with you, that was the last thing I wanted to hear, but there was nothing else left. I didn't want to utter that prayer, but my hope had run out. I shouted a desperate challenge to the universe and any god that might be there: "If there's a savior in this world, let me live to see tomorrow. If not, let me die tonight."

THE ANSWER

My next conscious memory is the rooster's morning cock-a-doodle. I wakened to a choir of harmonizing bird songs dancing around the house. The crisp air stung my cheeks and nose; my sluggish eyelids creaked open. Morning's first golden rays lit the room in crisscross patterns through slits in the bamboo wall. I exhaled a cloud of steam, which could only mean one thing: "I'm alive! I'm alive! I made it through the night!" And then, before the thought could fully sink in, my crazy Christian relative strolled up for the first time in over two years. He must have forgotten that I told him not to visit my house again. How odd that he just "happened" to show up the morning after my last-ditch prayer to Jesus. I didn't recognize it yet, but the Holy Spirit was working.

Seeing how weak I was, my Christian relative immediately went to town and brought back a pair of Christian Kachin nurses. My strength returned drop by drop as the bag of saline solution emptied into my body. All the while, I couldn't stop thinking about my deathbed prayer and God's direct answer. I had called out for a savior, the one the Christians told me about, and he clearly spared my life. The better I felt, the more I thought and the harder it was to sit still. What was I waiting for?

I sprang from my deathbed and marched to my Christian relative's house: "Give me a Bible!" I commanded like a military general. I didn't ask anything about Jesus—I didn't want to talk about it. I needed to read it for myself. And on the very first page, I found the answer to a question I had often pondered in the monastery.

The incredible things people built had always amazed me: skyscrapers, cars, and airplanes to name a few. Who gave people such incredible brains? I didn't find the answer in Buddhism. But right there, in the first chapter, this Bible said, "God created them *in his own image;* male and female *he created them.*" No wonder people invented such incredible things—*the greatest Inventor of all made them in his image!*

That might not seem like a novel concept if you grew up with a Bible—but I didn't. For me, this tiny sentence from the Bible's first page was a mighty spark—one that set my life on fire again! I immediately marched back to my Christian relative's house, this time without the military pomp. and plainly spoke my mind: "I want to be baptized." I laugh now because I didn't know anything about Jesus or salvation yet. All I knew was that Jesus had healed me and that the Christian God had made me. But at the time, that was enough. With those two simple truths, I shoved aside everything I had known and asked the Christians to dip me in water. It was a quick decision, but a good one—until I told my wife, that is. Can you guess what happened when she heard the big news?

GOD SHOT

God is orchestrating the details of every human life in every nation and religion, so that we will seek and find him—and he is not far away.

> *From one man he has made every nationality to live over the whole earth and has determined their appointed times and the boundaries of where they live. He did this so that they might seek God, and perhaps they might reach out and find him, though he is not far from each one of us.*
>
> (Acts 17:26–27)

PERSONAL REFLECTIONS

This is space to write personal discoveries, prayers, or anything else you find helpful. See this chapter's insights for mission in the back of the book or at jesusinthebuddhabelt.com.

2

Divorce or Miracle?

Shortly after my baptism, I felt like a kid running from danger in the monastery all over again. But this time I had done something right—not tried to steal the senior monk's cookies. The first person to get angry, of course, was my wife. She was still working in another village when I met the Christian God, but she had already found out what happened before I could tell her. When we finally saw each other, it wasn't a happy reunion. Her few choice words were hotter than a raw chili pepper: "Why the #*$%! did you go and worship the %@*&! Kachin god without telling me?" Her mouthful of hostility splatted on my cheekbone like a right hook. "Because I knew you wouldn't like it!" I snapped back with a quick verbal jab. Things went downhill from there and didn't come back up until a good while later—after another miracle. In the meantime, her blood was boiling and there was nothing I could do to cool it down; I couldn't even cool myself down.

The day I got baptized, the village was almost as angry as my wife. This was not surprising, but there *was* a big surprise that day—several others in the village came out to be baptized too! They had secretly wanted to worship Jesus but were afraid to do it alone. I don't blame them, either—for our simple-minded people, baptism is like dropping a bomb in the middle of the village. You can say you believe in Jesus all day long, but baptism is the concrete action that identifies you with him for good. When you go under the water, we get the picture—you have left your old life of Buddhism and started a new life with Jesus. Baptism is tangible evidence you've become a Christian and that makes you a village outcast forever.

There are rumors about baptism. People say the Christians keep dunking your head underwater until you see Jesus. This leaves us wondering: Will they drown you by repeated dunking if you don't see Jesus? The prospect of drowning aside, repeated dunking is a scary thought for rural mountain dwellers. Most of us have rarely had our heads underwater and don't know how to swim. The last thing we want is to have our heads forced underwater over and over again. Another common rumor is that Christians give gifts or money to coerce baptism. Even if a new believer overcomes their fears and goes through with baptism, the village will likely think they did it for financial gain—and nobody likes a sellout.

Of course, the other villagers were afraid to be baptized! I was too! But I guess the former head monk overcoming his fears gave them enough courage to come out of hiding, so we headed to the water together. This further enraged the village but did not change our course. The Ta'ang church was born that historic day in the face of great opposition, but we did not feel victorious for very long. I returned from the water to a group of snarling villagers circling my house with sticks and death threats. People have been killed in Ta'ang villages for getting baptized, and I didn't want to be one of them.

BAGS PACKED

My dad stood up at the next village gathering, cleared his throat, and shouted, "Aung is dead! He is no longer my son!" Words can't describe what happened inside me at that moment. My heart sank into my gut. My body froze. And my stone face barely held back the tears. All the villagers, all the monks, all the Ta'ang people rejecting me was nothing compared to the public rejection of this one person. "Daddy" was one of the first intelligible words I spoke as a child. Now the man I grew up using this special term of affection for had pre-published my obituary while I was still living. I couldn't show my face in the village; there was nothing to do but hide. Shame overwhelmed me, then fear. The villagers were extra angry about my conversion because I used to be their monk. I had taught them the Buddha's way and they worshipped me in return. My baptism betrayed all that. The village now considered me a backstabber. And in their minds, there was only one way to deal with this. They had to get rid of me. Thankfully, an old friend had mercy on me and leaked the news. But I felt powerless against the angry majority. What could I do?

Embarrassed and afraid, I decided not to go home that day. It was time to visit my crazy Christian relative. His house was the only safe place I could think of. He got on the phone and arranged for me to attend a Bible school several hours away. I needed to learn more about Jesus and the village needed time to cool down. Maybe a month of separation would be good for both of us. I packed my bags and asked my fuming wife for a promise before leaving. "If you don't submit the divorce papers while I'm gone, I'll do it for you when I get back ... if that's still what you want." I didn't want to lose my wife, but I couldn't hold her back if she was determined to leave. Thankfully, she accepted my offer. So off I went to Bible school like a newborn baby—hungry for the milk of God's word, not yet knowing I would have to drink it from a fire hydrant!

JESUS

The next month of Bible school served up more spiritual nutrition than I could digest. But it was still a godsend, even if it was overwhelming. Genesis 1:27 was the only Bible verse I knew when I got baptized. I had so much to learn about the Creator and his Son, Jesus. Learning about Jesus's miracles was interesting, but his death amazed me most. If Herod and Pilate found no sin in him, why was Jesus punished so cruelly? Where was the *Law of Karma*? This left me scratching my head, until the teacher explained: Jesus died for me. I knew I had sin; no arguments there. What I couldn't understand was how Jesus could pray, "Father, forgive them!" for the people who were killing him. The teacher said Jesus was talking about *me* too.

All Buddhists long for forgiveness and pray for it regularly: *"Aw-ka-tha, aw-ka-tha, aw-ka-tha ... "* But the Buddha teaches there is no escape from *karma*: "only cause and effect—you get what you deserve—no one else can be your substitute!" Jesus said something different: "But God shows his love for us in that while we were still sinners, Christ died for us" (Romans 5:8). Wow! What a difference!

Buddha said I had to pay for my own sin, but the Bible said God paid for my sin with the death of his son. Could God really love me that much? I struggled to wrap my mind around this strange new teaching. Jesus's love and sinless death for me—for my sin—went against all my brain's previous programming. I still don't fully understand it. But I do believe it. And it gives me peace.

But there's more ... after Jesus's surprising death, his story takes another shocking turn—he didn't stay dead! Are you kidding me? Jesus rose from the dead?! This is different from the Buddha's life experience and the way he taught others to cope with death. Consider this story from the Buddhist Scriptures:

> A woman named *Kisa Gotami* had an only son, whom she loved dearly. When the son died at a young age, his grieving mother frantically carried his body around the village seeking medicine to restore his life. After no one could resurrect her lifeless son, someone suggested asking the Buddha for help. "Please, give me medicine to bring my son back to life!" *Kisa Gotami* pleaded. "Bring me a mustard seed and I will help," replied the Buddha. "But the mustard seed must come from a house that has not experienced death." After searching many houses, *Kisa Gotami* realized the Buddha's request was impossible—every house had experienced death. She would have to accept it too. With this new realization, she buried her son and became the Buddha's disciple.

The Buddha taught Kisa Gotami a wise lesson on the universality of death—but he could not raise her son from the dead. Jesus, on the other hand, raised several people from the dead. He even rose from the dead himself and promised to resurrect his followers one day too! The power of Jesus over death was something I did not find in Buddhism. It blew my mind and filled my heart. Jesus was the first person to do both of these things. My mind drifted back to my deathbed prayer just a few months earlier. I had experienced Jesus's power over death in the bamboo hut that night. But in my case, he used his power before the fact—to prevent death—rather than afterward, to resurrect it.

One more surprise from my fire hydrant month of Bible school: Despite all that Jesus has already done, he is not finished yet. Jesus promised to come back one day. He will deal out justice, dry our tears, and rule as king forever in the new heavens and new earth—no more aging, sickness, or death! The cessation of suffering is Buddhism's ultimate goal; we call it *nirvana*. *Nirvana* is compared to a candle burning out. When the wick is extinguished, there's nothing left—nothing bad, nothing good— just total annihilation. That's the Buddhist hope of *nirvana*. I could hardly believe how beautifully Jesus's future kingdom promised to satisfy this hope, but Jesus's kingdom was much better! Not only did he promise the end of suffering, Jesus also promised enduring happiness with him forever. This is what all Buddhists are hoping for deep down—we just don't know that Jesus is the one who gives it. This news was too good to keep to myself. So when I heard that Jesus sent his followers to tell the good news of salvation everywhere, I signed up immediately! My people had hated Jesus all these years without even knowing him. And look what they were missing! Maybe God could use me to change that.

It felt like my Bible school days were just getting started when they ended. I wasn't ready to leave that brief moment of peace and enlightenment yet. I also wasn't ready to go home and face the impending storm. But I had to do both. How would my wife and the village respond? I had a few morbid guesses but would have to go home to get the answer.

REUNION

After winding and bumping for hours on a rickety bus, I wound and bumped for hours on a rickety motorcycle. That eventually got me back to the village. *What would my wife say? Would she follow through on the divorce threat? Or would things change?* There was only one way to find out. Step by slow step, I soberly climbed the wood-plank stairway of our humble home. Her worn-out flip-flops sat on the elevated front porch near the doorway as usual. I kicked my flip-flops off and nudged them next to hers with a sick feeling rising in my gut. The last step across the threshold took all the courage I could muster. I swallowed hard, uttered a silent prayer, and walked into something entirely unexpected. Instead of an angry wife, I found a subdued one. The ill health of our little son had taken its toll on her. He got sick shortly after I left for Bible school, and his health had steadily declined since then. My poor wife had tried everything in her power to get help, but despite the best doctors and medicine we could afford, our boy showed no improvement. We feared that our dear son was on the all-too-familiar village trail of sickness that ends in death.

Then, before I even had time to sit, my wife made a jarring proposition: "If your God can heal our son, I'll become a Christian too." What a happy thought! I'd love for my wife to become a Christian! But if the doctors couldn't help our son, what could I do? My wife's offer was based on a condition I could not control. I didn't know what to do, but I remembered that Jesus had healed blind and lame people—even raised some from the dead. Hadn't he saved me from impending death too? I looked deep into my wife's weary eyes, down at my son, then back to her. Maybe I could try asking Jesus for help, although I doubted he'd listen. I didn't even know all the fancy prayer words.

But with nowhere else to turn, I tenderly scooped up my son, walked out the front door, and shuffled down the steps. I kept walking down the mountain, through the tea fields, and into the forest until there was no one but me, my sick son, and Almighty God. My chin started quivering before I could open my mouth. Soon, there was no hiding it—my whole body was shaking. I could not stop the tears. The emotion had to run its course down my chiseled cheeks. Finally, I regained enough composure to muster a few simple words: "God, this is your son. I put him in your hands." That was it. I didn't know what else to say.

No fire came down from heaven. I didn't know if I'd even been heard. But after walking aimlessly in the forest for an eternal half hour, I turned home, having done all I could. Did Jesus see me? Did he care? Would he heal my dying son? My eyes glanced back and forth between the path in front of me and the limp child in my arms as my feet plodded homeward. Finally, I made it back to the wood-plank steps and worn-out flip-flops. I crossed the threshold with my head hung low one more time, carrying a sick son with no sign of improvement.

Jesus didn't answer our prayer that day—*he did it at night while we were sleeping!* In the morning—I can't even tell you now without a huge smile stretching across my face—the most amazing thing happened. My son sat up in bed. He just sat up like his normal, healthy self! Soon he was out of bed eating and playing. His mom and I looked at each other in disbelief. We knew what had happened. Our death-ridden little boy had just sat up in bed. Yesterday it was his *death*bed. Today it was just his bed—no more death. It seemed too good to be true, but it was true—our precious son had just been healed by a last-ditch prayer to Jesus!

NEW BEGINNINGS

For the moment, we didn't talk much about the miraculous healing we had just seen—neither one of us really knew what to say about it. But later, when I asked my wife if she still wanted a divorce, I saw how much this answer to prayer had changed her perspective on Jesus. Her poker face melted into a schoolgirl grin: "I want to be baptized too." This was an even bigger miracle than the one I had just seen! In front of my very eyes, my proud Ta'ang-Buddhist wife was trading in everything she had ever known to follow a God she had hated and cursed until now. This was the third time I experienced Jesus do the impossible.

On the day of my wife's baptism, we became the first Ta'ang Christian couple we knew of. What joy! What relief! Instead of a broken marriage, our family was together—and stronger than ever! We now knew our Creator and had the help of Jesus, our Savior, who forgave our sins, healed our sicknesses, and guaranteed our future. Then an unwelcome visitor stomped in and slapped joy in the face with an eviction notice. Just like that, we were kicked out of the village!

While preparing for homelessness, God stepped in and made a way where there was none. Some Christian brothers and sisters from another tribe heard our story and offered us a small plot of land. It was not a land flowing with milk and honey—it didn't even have a house on it—but we could build one. So we silently said goodbye to the little bamboo hut where our children were born and our vegetables were still growing. Our families didn't even bid us farewell. Humanly speaking, we were now orphans.

As we held our things and took one last look at our former home, God brought the story of the exodus to mind. His people had to leave in a hurry when Moses brought them out of Egypt. I guess our family could leave in a hurry too. This was our Exodus. But it didn't feel like victory, and this didn't look like the promised land. I guess the wilderness would come first for us too. But what difficulties would we face? And how long would we have to wander? We'll save those stories for another day and another pot of tea. For now, I'll just say that the difficulties were many, but God's grace was more.

REFLECTIONS

Years later, I can honestly say that life following Jesus hasn't been easy. I've been threatened with death, beaten with sticks, disowned by my family, and kicked out of the village for it. I went from first to last, before knowing that the last would be first. In some ways I still haven't experienced the good side of that paradox yet. But when the monastic authorities offered me a high price to return to Buddhism, I didn't need to discuss it with anybody. I didn't need to compare my financial prospects or think it over. My mouth just calmly opened and let out an unrehearsed sentence that came as naturally as breathing: "Jesus gave me eternal life. What compares with that?"

My life used to be a complicated mess of religious rules that I couldn't keep and superstitious rituals that didn't help. I did anything and everything I could to keep the bad at bay and try to grab some luck. "Don't travel on this day. Don't have a wedding on that day. Pay the astrologer for advice when business is bad. Make an offering when you're sick. Appease this spirit by pouring water. Don't irritate that spirit by walking under a tree. Count your rosary beads. Meditate. Cease desire. Do the Buddha's works. And always, always make donations." We carefully tried to do all that, hoping things would work out—in this life *and* the next—all the while knowing deep down, they would not. There is no promise, no guarantee, no real basis for hope.

Following Jesus hasn't made my life easy, but it has made it simpler. I'm not drowning in dead rules and rituals anymore, no more living in fear and grasping for luck. I have quit the works-based manipulation tactics and accepted Jesus's invitation: "Come to me, all who are weary and carry heavy burdens, and I will give you rest." That's good news! Whether I'm sick or hungry, business is bad, or relationships are broken—whatever the situation—Jesus is with me. He knows what I need, and that's enough. All I have to do is ask. He doesn't always do what I ask, but he hears me, and he helps me. He's a good Father and a good Shepherd.

I don't know how my simple answer about Jesus hit the monastic leaders' ears that day. Maybe they wouldn't let it in, and I guess that's okay—it took me years to finally listen. But I hope one day they will reach the end of themselves like I did—I think that's the only way. Then, at the end of self-reliance, maybe they will open their ears and hear the voice that's always been there, calling to them in love. Maybe it will be the only thing left they can hear. And then, just maybe, they'll do the unthinkable and call out to Jesus like I did! It only takes a tiny spark to set a whole forest on fire. I know this from personal experience. My crazy Christian relative knew it before me. And many others knew it before him.

I think that's how the good news works—one spark ignites a fire that continues to spread from one person to another. It passed to me from a crazy Christian relative—thank God!

I wouldn't be here without him. It's about time I introduce you to Thant and the surprising people that he got the fire from—the crazy Christians. For this part of the story you'll need a pair of Ta'ang glasses, but don't worry, I brought an extra pair.

GOD SHOT

Jesus is the greatest treasure—and he is worth exchanging everything else, if necessary, to get.

> *The kingdom of heaven is like treasure, buried in a field, that a man found and reburied. Then in his joy he goes and sells everything he has and buys that field.*
>
> (Matthew 13:44)

PERSONAL REFLECTIONS

This is space to write personal discoveries, prayers, or anything else you find helpful. See this chapter's insights for mission in the back of the book or at jesusinthebuddhabelt.com.

3
Thant and the Crazy Christians

I guess Almighty God could zap people into his kingdom all by himself if he wanted. But that's not how it happened for me. God used another person to bring me from darkness to light, a person I didn't like very much—my crazy Christian in-law. Remember Thant? Thant mysteriously appeared at my house the morning I shouldn't have woken up, gave me a Bible when I was looking for God, and sent me to safety when I needed to get lost. I want you to meet Thant because he helped me come to know Jesus. He also happens to be a very interesting character—interesting in one way before I knew Jesus, and interesting in a different way now. I never thought I'd have such a pendulum swing about a person, but nowadays, I think I love Thant even more than I hated him back then. Why did I hate Thant so much before I became a Christian? Let me tell you.

Thant was Ta'ang—he was born that way just like the rest of us. But Thant was not like the rest of us. He *was* like us when we were growing up, even into early adulthood. Then, he went off the deep end. Thant threw away his Ta'ang identity by marrying a foreign lady and worshipping her foreign god. That was the point of no return, the moment our people unanimously wrote him off as a backstabber. To us, Thant was Kachin now: a foreigner and Christian like his wife. How could this man live with himself? I understand now because I have walked the trail behind him. But back then I was baffled. We all were. We viewed Thant the only way we could—through the Ta'ang glasses we were wearing. My view of him only changed when I got a new prescription.

Have you ever seen the toy glasses that reveal hidden images? The ones with white paper frames and red plastic lenses? A friend once let me look through a pair. They came with a book of specially designed pictures that looked like a mishmash of random colors and shapes until you put on the glasses. Then, previously hidden images appeared—they were there all along—but invisible without the glasses. That's what I mean by Ta'ang glasses: the invisible lenses that color my people's view of the world. You need a pair to properly understand Thant's story; otherwise, you won't see the hidden images through the mishmash.

Here, try these on. Do they fit okay? Now, before looking at anything else through your new Ta'ang glasses, first take a look in the mirror. The first thing the glasses change is how you view yourself. What do you see? When I look in the mirror through Ta'ang glasses I see a man. A Ta'ang man. A Ta'ang-Buddhist man. That's what I've seen every day since my Ta'ang-Buddhist mother and Ta'ang-Buddhist father brought me and my seven Ta'ang-Buddhist siblings into the world. Everybody in our Ta'ang-Buddhist village sees the same thing I do—except some are women and children, of course. Age and gender aside, we all see the same thing in the mirror—Ta'ang and Buddhist. Our parents and their parents saw it too for as many generations as we can remember. We didn't choose to be Ta'ang-Buddhist. We didn't choose it, and we can't un-choose it. That's just how it is—and always will be.

I told you our people are concrete. Think of it like this: What ingredients do you mix to get mud? Water and dirt, right? What do you mix to get a cup of tea? Hot water and tea leaves. Easy. Then what would you mix to make me and the rest of my people? Ta'ang and Buddhist. It's that simple. Ta'ang-Buddhist parents make Ta'ang-Buddhist children, and the pattern repeats without end. Laws of the universe don't change. Are you starting to understand what Ta'ang people see in the mirror? These are not things we chose and they are not things we can change. We were born Ta'ang-Buddhist and we will die that way—unless and until we see Jesus looking over our shoulder in the mirror.

THE PROBLEM WITH CHRISTIANS

Here's another thing that will come into focus through your new pair of Ta'ang glasses: Christians are atheists. That's probably not how you're used to thinking of them, but let me explain. Buddhists have gods. They're on a platform in every temple, a shelf in every home. Some gods are big, some are small—but images of the Buddha are everywhere—you can see and touch them. Where are the Christian gods? Can you see and touch them? They say they have one god and he's invisible. What kind of god is that? If I tried to sell you an invisible car, would you buy it? Of course not! Who would? People want a car they can see, touch, and drive—that's how you get somewhere. Christians may as well be driving a car you can't see.

If you've still got your Ta'ang glasses on, you'll see another problem with Christians: they believe their god forgives them. It sounds great to be forgiven until you realize how much sin it causes. The *Law of Karma* keeps my people afraid to sin. It's not that we don't sin—we do—we just know there's no escaping sin's consequences. You do good; you get good. You do bad; you get bad. That's *karma*. You don't do bad and get good in return—*unless* you're a Christian—they say you can. That's why some Christians are worse drunkards, wife-beaters, and gossips than us. Their invisible god forgives sin, leaving no restraint against it. They don't believe in the *Law of Karma*. And every Buddhist knows that's a sure ticket straight to hell.

These are a few issues coloring the Ta'ang view of things. Can you see why we were so angry and bewildered when Thant married a Kachin Christian lady? He chose the un-choosable—betraying his mother, father, brothers, sisters, all of us. He betrayed the man in the mirror too—and all just to get a woman! We knew it wouldn't last—it couldn't. Thant's actions were like dyeing your hair a different color. It looks real for a while, but the natural color eventually returns. It's a temporary illusion—something the Buddha teaches us to avoid at all costs.

Through my highly esteemed pair of Ta'ang glasses, Thant was a crazy Christian backstabber. That's why I couldn't stand to see his face anymore, and I didn't see it for years—until the morning after Jesus saved my life. Since then, I've seen Thant often, and I'm now quite happy about it ... most of the time.

CAUSE AND EFFECT IN ACTION

Back to Thant's story. After he became a Christian, we kicked him out of the village. The Buddhist worldview is ruled by the *Law of Cause and Effect*—the two are everywhere intertwined and cyclical. You won't find one without the other. Thant betrayed his family, village, and people; that's the cause. Then, his life was made miserable; that's the effect. Ta'ang people are experts at ridding a village of dissension. It's easy. You just disown a person, publicly shame them, and force them to leave. It works nearly every time.

We threw these tried-and-true tactics at Thant and our plan worked; he soon left the village with his foreign wife and two young children. I don't know if they even had a blanket to share on that first chilly night under the stars. They had no shelter, just a spot outside the village in the open air, where they gathered firewood and hoped to keep warm through the night. At the time, I couldn't feel sorry for them—it was the *Law of Cause and Effect*. I wondered what Thant thought about his invisible god that night. Where was his god now? And was he worth all the trouble?

The village hoped our unified response would teach Thant a lesson, but it didn't. A group of Christians soon came to the rescue and helped his family find a new place to live. He probably thought his god had saved them. Whatever the case, he was out of the village and slowly fading from our minds. Then, just as things returned to normal, Thant showed up in the village again. How dare he return to the village that had kicked him out! He should have been ashamed for life. But there he was, head held high and smiling. What happened next is even more amazing. Thant didn't just visit one village; he started a campaign to spread his new religion all over the area. He was dead set on getting everybody to join him in worshipping Jesus!

We already had lots of reasons to hate Thant. He had shamed our elders, ancestors, and everything else for his invisible god! But now, as if his personal departure from our people wasn't enough, Thant started a mission to turn us all into backstabbing Christians just like him! What nerve! Thant still hadn't learned the lessons our people were trying to teach him, and it was starting to look like he never would.

PREACHER OF GOOD NEWS

Thant wasn't the first person to preach the "good news" in a Ta'ang village. The Kachin came first, but their methods were different than Thant's. Ta'ang kids loved Kachin songs, and Ta'ang adults loved the gifts of rice, clothing, and other useful items. Sure, the Kachin sang and talked about Jesus, but it was all in *their* language—*not ours*. Who doesn't love free food and education for their children? We did what they wanted while they were in the village, but things went back to normal the moment they left. Thant, on the other hand, didn't babysit our kids. He didn't give us gifts either. More importantly, he didn't speak a foreign language. Thant spoke and sang Jesus's words in our native Ta'ang language. That's a different matter entirely! And that's what got the village boiling.

Being and speaking Ta'ang, Thant received a drastically different response than the gift-giving, foreign-speaking Kachin. We politely courted the Kachin and their gifts, but explicitly told Thant we had no use for him and his atheist religion. Our people cursed, threatened, and at least once, beat him for it. In the face of all this, Thant's response was shocking. He did not run away. He did not respond with anger or hate. "They hate me," he said, "but I love them." That was Thant's smiling response to the village leaders who kicked him out and threatened his death. You would have thought he was talking about a cute younger sibling who could do no harm, not grown adults who posed real danger. I couldn't understand Thant's simple response of love, but it spoke more to me than a thousand pages in a thousand books. It gives me goosebumps even now.

PARALYZING LOVE

There's something else about Thant that amazed me back then. His normal pattern was to ask the village leader's permission before preaching the good news. This seemed like a good strategy to bypass persecution. If you didn't ask first, the village leader could cause trouble later. If he granted permission, on the other hand, no one could stop you. Unfortunately, the village leaders typically said no.

Most of the village leaders emphatically told Thant not to bring his foreign religion under their jurisdiction. In that case, Thant would move on in search of somewhere more receptive, "shaking the dust," as Jesus said. When his request was rejected by a village leader, that was usually the end of it. Thant would leave the village, and they would miss their chance to hear the good news. One village rejection, though, had a different ending.

This particular occasion began like many others. Thant requested the village leader's permission to share the message of Jesus. When the village leader said no, Thant shook the dust off his feet and continued looking for a more receptive place. This time, though, an interesting report came a few days later—the village leader had become paralyzed since Thant's departure. The village leader did not believe in accidents and attributed his paralysis to the vengeance of Thant's god. Surely he was being punished for blockading the message of Jesus!

The only logical thing the village leader could do now was ask Thant to come back and pray for him. Thant returned and prayed for the village leader's healing. Can you guess what happened next? The village leader made a quick recovery. That's the good part. The bad part is that he still wouldn't let Thant preach the good news in his village. Then, a short time later, the village leader died an unnatural death. My stunned people were left with no good explanation—except for the power of Jesus, foreign god of the Kachin.

The thing that bothered me and most of my people, at the time, was how powerful this incident made the Kachin god look. Power is not strange to us. Spirit mediums, monks, astrologers—they all have power. We pray and perform rituals to manipulate this power, but none of our familiar power sources can do what the Kachin god did. That bothered us because we didn't like this strange, foreign god very much. Honestly, we were all at least a little afraid. It looked like this god was more powerful than the others, but what were we supposed to do? We couldn't worship him without abandoning everything we knew—and none of us were ready to do that.

We all secretly stood in awe of Jesus for a brief moment, but he was still a long way in the distance—right where we wanted him. We didn't want Jesus to come close; neither did we want to move close to him. Even if we did, how could we? It's like we were standing on top of one mountain looking at another in the distance. It's easy to see the other mountain from where you stand, even admire its beauty. The problem is there's a jungle in between. You can't get to the other mountain without passing through the jungle—and to do that, you need a path.

At the time, my people were starting to see a distant, blurry picture of Jesus across the jungle, but we still couldn't see a path to him. For some of us though, that was about to change. And it changed because someone showed us a way that we previously could not see (interesting what you see when you change glasses). Would you like to know some of the paths that led our Ta'ang-Buddhist people across the jungle to Jesus? I'm betting they're different than the paths in your country. But I'm also betting they illuminate your journey in some surprising ways. Maybe they'll even help you reveal a path for someone else to follow.

GOD SHOT

God often does not spare his people from persecution, but instead uses persecution to produce maturity in their lives and validate their gospel witness.

> *Just one thing: As citizens of heaven, live your life worthy of the gospel of Christ. Then, whether I come and see you or am absent, I will hear about you that you are standing firm in one spirit, in one accord, contending together for the faith of the gospel, not being frightened in any way by your opponents. This is a sign of destruction for them, but of your salvation—and this is from God. For it has been granted to you on Christ's behalf not only to believe in him, but also to suffer for him, since you are engaged in the same struggle that you saw I had and now hear that I have.*
>
> (Phil 1:27–30)

PERSONAL REFLECTIONS

This is space to write personal discoveries, prayers, or anything else you find helpful. See this chapter's insights for mission in the back of the book or at jesusinthebuddhabelt.com.

4
Going Deeper: Trail Guides to Jesus

Earlier, I described the narrow dirt trail that leads to my obscure mountain village. There are no maps, no street signs, no cell phone signals to show the way. It's an impossible journey without a guide—and very few people know the way. Reverse that image and you'll understand how hard it is for my people to find Jesus. Most of us have never seen a Bible. We don't have churches in our villages. The Buddhist monks constantly inoculate us against the truth. And our whole society thinks changing religion means betraying our people. No, my people are not going to stumble across the Jesus trail on our own. Everything in our lives is keeping us from it. How would we ever find Jesus without a guide? And how few guides there are! Lord, send us more guides!

By God's grace, though, a few unique individuals have shown my people the way of Jesus. These guides have suffered a lot, but a scattered handful of Ta'ang Jesus followers has resulted from their efforts. Each pioneer Ta'ang Christian's story is different, but most of them share two things in common: 1) a personal experience of Jesus's power through prayer and 2) an intelligible explanation of the gospel. Most of the Buddhist background believers I know have experienced these elements too, even from other ethnic groups.

The Ta'ang, like most Myanmar people, are concrete. We are not likely to be interested in Jesus until we experience his power. This is usually what gets our attention in the beginning. Experiencing his power is step one. Then we will probably listen to an explanation of Jesus's message; this is step two. Most of us don't get to step two without step one. When people go straight to step two and explain a lot of things about Jesus, we usually aren't interested. Step one is important for many of us, but after step one, there *must* be someone to explain—otherwise, how can we know the way of Jesus? That's where the guides come in. Here are a few ways they have led us to Jesus.

NOT MY DAD

Anyone aspiring to share the good news with my people needs to know what the name "Jesus" triggers in our minds. Remember yourself as a child for a moment. Imagine someone you don't know walks up with a picture of a strange, foreign man with an odd name. "Here's your dad," he says. "He's waiting for you to come to him." How would you react? Seeing no resemblance between the picture and the man you know as Father, you would probably scream, "No! That's *not* my dad!" and run away. For the Ta'ang, and most other people in Myanmar, Buddha is the only dad they know. So don't expect them to quickly change their minds and call this newly introduced foreigner "Dad."

My people have been happily drawing water from the Buddha's well for a thousand years and see no need to change. From the Buddha's well, they have drawn their deepest moral and existential lessons: right and wrong, the cause of suffering, the way out of suffering, and *karma's* effects on past and future reincarnations. They highly esteem this ancient well and the water they draw from it. Any suggestion of dumping it in exchange for something else is highly offensive. Their attitude toward your gospel invitation will probably be like the Samaritan woman Jesus offered living water to: "Are you greater than our father who dug this well?" Our people will not openly say it, though. They'll just smile and nod their heads while thinking it. As far as most of our Myanmar people are concerned, Buddha is their father—and they are proud of it. So when you walk in quoting the Bible, ask them to call Jesus "Dad," and tell them to drink his water, they won't be quick to do it. They have happily drunk from the Buddha's well too long for that.

I'm not saying living water isn't better than what my people currently have—it *is* better. I'm not saying God's Word doesn't have the power to transform lives—it *certainly* does. I am just telling you how my people view things. That can be the difference between helping someone understand how good a thing is and hitting them on the head with it. You won't know how to most effectively wield the power of Jesus's words until you listen and understand first. Scratching someone where they don't itch makes an enemy. Scratching someone where they *do* itch makes a friend—and brings much-needed relief. That's what my people are looking for: friends who bring relief, people who listen and understand. Once they see you that way, your message will have a better chance of getting through.

THE SUM OF BUDDHISM

If you're open to listening and learning from our Buddhist brothers and sisters (so that you can more effectively share Jesus with them), here's a place to start: I wore the monk robe for years, and what did I find in the Lord Buddha's Scriptures? Three Books of Discourse (*Sutta*), five Books of Monastic Order (*Vinaya*), and seven Books of Higher Knowledge (*Abhidharma*)—that's the totality of the Buddhist Scriptures. The commentaries are endless, but that's all the Scriptures. King Anawrata and the monk Arahan spread these Three Baskets of teaching (*Tipitaka*) throughout Myanmar in the eleventh century AD. These men dug the wells of Buddhism in our country.

What is the sum of teaching in the Three Baskets of Buddhist Scripture we received? I will sum it all up for you in a few short words: works of the law. All of the Scriptures boil down to this one thing—you must do the works of the law to attain enlightenment, *nirvana*, the cessation of suffering. That's the end goal of Buddhism, and works are the way to get there. Prince Gautama left the palace for the forest and did the works for six years to attain enlightenment and become a Buddha.

Of course, Prince Gautama's enlightenment would have never been possible without the accumulated merit and skill carried over from previous lives. After thousands of lifetimes doing good works, Prince Gautama finally attained enlightenment and became a god, or Buddha. That's the way of Buddhism—do the works to get the reward. If you can't do the works, try again and again and again. The particulars of the works are methodically spelled out in the Noble Eightfold Path, but the biggest part is meditation.

MEDITATION AND THE SAVIOR

In my days as a monk, I would sit down to do meditation. I was hot and sweating, my mind running all over the place—every night—it's crazy! Just like the Buddha said, "Sinners are crazy." In meditation, you focus on your breath. Breathe in; breathe out. Just as you're doing that, your foot starts hurting. Then you get an itch—you want to scratch it so badly! Then along comes a mosquito. You fear being bitten, but don't dare break a commandment to take its life: "From taking life ... I will refrain." You recite the precept as the mosquito sticks you in the arm. In a moment you're itching, and just like that the fire of anger is raging. Insanity! What good is it all?

I spent nine years that way! For what? It was a waste of time with no reward. In winter, everybody bundled up in jackets and hats, while I walked around shivering with a bald head. I thought to myself, "I've got a shaved head, but I can't do the works of the Buddha. What's the point? All I've gotten is a cold head!" Even steel—hard as it is—rusts and gets weak with time. And people are weaker than steel. We can't take the heat. We can't take the cold. We can't take anything. As hard as I tried, it just wasn't happening. I couldn't do all the works required by the Buddha's teaching—I'm convinced no one can! For me, that discovery was the logical end of Buddhism.

Buddhism is the way of self-reliance, the way of works, the way of meditation—and ultimately the way of despair for those who truly understand it. Most of our Buddhist brothers and sisters have not yet reached this conclusion. They have wives and children and jobs—no time for meditation! Most of them live on the lower plane just trying to do more good than bad, hoping for a better reincarnation so they can try and try and try and try again. Don't even talk about *nirvana*—it's a pipe dream! Once I came to this discovery, there was nothing left to do but leave the monastery.

I'm telling you about my experience in the monastery so you'll know the logical end of the Buddha's way. Most people are too busy looking for love and dollars to discover this for themselves, but anyone who follows Buddhist teaching to its logical conclusion will understand their total inability to keep all the requirements. This shows our need for a savior. A savior is the only way out of suffering—and where will you find a savior? Buddha does not claim to be a savior; Mohammed does not claim to be a savior; Krishna does not claim to be a savior. All these religious leaders teach some form of karma—action and reaction, you get what you deserve. The only one I have found who claims to be a savior is Jesus. The Scriptures say Jesus died for our sins and God raised him from the dead—something no other religion claims. I used to think this was Western nonsense, but now I believe it because I have tasted and seen it in my own experience. Jesus has answered my prayers and my biggest questions in a way that Buddhism did not. Buddhism showed me a path out of suffering that I couldn't walk; Jesus showed me that he is the Path, he is the Truth, he is the Life—and no one can come to the Almighty Father except through him. God's grace is so huge! Endless words of praise cannot say enough!

DROWNING MAN

Imagine you're hiking through the woods and come across a man who has fallen into deep water. He frantically flails his arms and legs, screaming at the top of his lungs, "Help! Help!" The man obviously can't swim and will die soon without intervention. What does this man need? Does it help to say, "Hey! Move your arms like this. Kick your feet like that?" No. He's a bit too busy drowning for a swim lesson at the moment. Panicked, battling for every breath, and exhausted from keeping afloat, there's no chance a swim lesson will work now—and the clock is ticking. The drowning man doesn't have the ability or time to learn a new skill while he's drowning.

Offering a swim lesson is one approach to the drowning man's problem—but it's not a helpful one. Sure, if he could do what the swim coach said, everything would work out fine. The problem is, he cannot. The offer of a swim lesson is like religion: "Do this and you'll gain a reward; refrain from that and you'll escape punishment." Religion tells you the good works to do and the sins to avoid, along with their corresponding rewards and punishments—that's all. The doing and refraining is up to you. There's no one to do it for you, no one to help—nowhere to turn for refuge but yourself. Instruction is a beautiful thing if you can follow along and do it, but it isn't much use to a drowning man.

A drowning man doesn't need a swim lesson—he needs someone to pull him out with a rope! That's the way of Jesus. He knows we will never be able to keep all the "dos" and "don'ts" of the law. If it's left up to our self-effort and skill alone, the statistical probability of survival is a simple calculation—0.000 percent—we all drown. Then Jesus comes along and changes the statistics. He sees us and is moved with compassion. Jesus tosses in a rope and pulls us safely back to shore—rescuing us from certain death! That's what drowning people need; that's what sinners need. That's what we all need because that's who we all are! This is a path you can lead our Buddhist brothers and sisters to Jesus on.

TOTE-SEE-DOE

Buddhists have a hard time understanding how Jesus's death and resurrection apply to us. We are taught from the beginning that there is no creator, no higher power, no one to rely on but ourselves. "What Jesus did is great," we think, "but it has nothing to do with me. I must do for myself." The children's game *tote-see-doe* can create a path for Buddhists to escape this rut of thinking and understand how Jesus can set us free, despite our inability to keep the Law.

Tote-see-doe is played by two opposing teams on a court of dirt or pavement. The defensive players are only allowed to move along the court's dividing lines; they try to eliminate the other team by tagging them out. The offensive players have unrestricted movement on the court; they try to reach the other side without being tagged by defenders. If one of the offensive team's players makes it to the other end of the court without being tagged, the offense gets a point. After both teams take a turn, the team with the most points wins.

Tote-see-doe is great fun to watch, especially with a crowd of rowdy children. The chatter of sideline cheering grows louder as the game continues, each enthralled fan determined to boost her friends to victory by raising her voice above the rest. Powered by adrenaline and fanfare, the players channel all their mental and physical energy trying to win the game. The atmosphere is electric! Each tag and narrow escape is exciting to watch, but the unquestionable climax is when an offensive player slips past the final defender and scores the winning point. In this moment of glory, the offensive team and spectators spontaneously erupt in celebration and the defensive players hang their heads in defeat.

Sometimes only one player may cross the finish line in a whole game, with everyone else being tagged out. In this case, all the tagged players would lose if it was based on their own performance. But the winning team celebrates victory—not because of what each individual has done—but because one of their teammates made it to the other side *for them*. They are winners by association, not by their own virtue. One person has gained victory for them all!

Tote-see-doe shows us the way of Jesus. We couldn't do the works of the law on our own. We couldn't escape the cycle of sin and suffering on our own. Then Jesus came and did what we could not! In his sinless life, death for our sins, and victorious resurrection, Jesus made it to the other side. And he invites us all to join his team and share his victory. We cannot win by our own virtue, but we can win by association with Jesus!

MY BROTHER'S FUNERAL

I discovered another path to Jesus at my brother's funeral. When I first became a Christian, I treated the Buddhist monastery like a mean dog. I didn't throw rocks at it; I just kept a safe distance.

But when my little brother died, what could I do? I had to attend his funeral, so I hoped for the best, braced for the worst, put on my traditional Ta'ang suit and went. I kept my head low, hoping to blend in, but hope can't hide a black fly on a white wall. Everybody's eyes were glued to me, and they all wanted to swat the fly. I pretended not to know they were staring until a blunt, elderly woman could no longer restrain herself. She walked up and smacked me—at least that's what her verbal assault felt like. "I remember what you used to teach from this monastery," she began, preparing to shame me in front of the eager crowd of spectators. Thankfully, the words that came to me in that moment were "turn the other cheek" instead of "cause and effect."

I didn't know what to say to this woman, but God must have given me the words. "What do you mean?" I calmly replied. "You warned us about imitation Buddhists, but now you're a Christian," she continued. Realizing this might be an opportunity to share the good news, I asked her, "Do you know what that means?" She was silent. "Do you know the Five Precepts?" I continued, before rapid-fire quoting them to her in Pali language like I had done so many times from this very monastery:

> From taking life ... I will refrain.
> From taking what is not given ... I will refrain.
> From sensuous misconduct ... I will refrain.
> From untruthful speech ... I will refrain.
> From harmful drugs and alcohol ... I will refrain.

The look on the lady's face started to change. With growing boldness I went on, "A person who can't keep the Five Precepts—that's an imitation Buddhist. It has nothing to do with Christians." At this point, the tables had clearly turned in my direction. Nobody watching dared utter a word. They all knew what I said was true: none of them could keep the Buddha's teaching. I slowly craned my neck away from the woman and returned the audience's gazes. I already had their full attention, but now they were listening in a different kind of way.

Before the funeral I had noticed some of the villagers guarding my brother's body. They do this from fear of the spiritual realm.

Ghosts, spirits, and demons are as common in village life as rain and crops. Everyone knows they are present, even if we don't know when and where they'll appear—and that keeps most of us afraid. I said this, hoping to use it as a bridge to Jesus: "You were guarding my brother's body, because you were afraid his spirit would leave. We all know that people's spirits leave their bodies when they die. Some spirits become guardians of the village, the house, etc." Their eyes agreed, and they wondered what I would say next.

"Go into the market and what will you find?" I continued. "Living and dead animals for sale. You can sell an animal whether it's alive or dead, because an animal doesn't have a spirit. But how about people? You can sell a living person for a good price, but if you take a human corpse into the market, who's going to buy it? No one. People are like animals in some ways, but in this way we're different: living people have spirits. Nobody will buy a human corpse in the market, because it has no value once the spirit has departed." I paused to let this sink in.

The audience had now scooted to the edge of their seats. I continued: "People leave the house and go to work in the morning, but they don't stay at work forever. In the evening they come back home. That's a picture of our lives. We have all left home and are now at work for a short time. When evening comes, we will have to return home. The problem is that many of us don't know where we came from, so we don't know the way home. When God breathed life into Adam and Eve, he gave them a spirit. One day that spirit must return to him. If we don't know where it came from and don't know the way home, we are lost." I paused again before concluding: "We need to know the way home to the God who made our spirits."

I didn't do an altar call at the Buddhist monastery that day. Everyone listening knew I followed Jesus, and they knew where to find me if they wanted to learn more. It was enough for that day. I think those were the words God wanted me to say. Maybe those words cracked someone's hard exterior enough for a little light to shine through. That's a good first step for most of us: something old cracking so something new can come in—light that can lead us down the path to Jesus—*if* we are willing to go.

GOD SHOT

God did not give the Law to make us right with him, but to reveal our sin and need for a savior—so that we might be made right with him by faith in Jesus—the only perfect Law Keeper.

> *For no one will be justified in his sight by the works of the law, because the knowledge of sin comes through the law. But now, apart from the law, the righteousness of God has been revealed, attested by the Law and the Prophets. The righteousness of God is through faith in Jesus Christ to all who believe, since there is no distinction. For all have sinned and fall short of the glory of God; they are justified freely by his grace through the redemption that is in Christ Jesus.*
>
> (Rom 3:20–24)

PERSONAL REFLECTIONS

This is space to write personal discoveries, prayers, or anything else you find helpful. See this chapter's insights for mission in the back of the book or at jesusinthebuddhabelt.com.

DISCUSSION AND PRAYER GUIDE

This was the final chapter in Aung's story. See the Discussion and Prayer Guide in the back of this book for deeper personal or group reflection or scan the QR code for an online version.

jesusinthebuddhabelt.com
Also scan this QR code to:

 SHARE your thoughts or ask a question

 EXPLORE the topics of this book further with free articles, photos, videos, and recipes

 CONNECT with ongoing mission initiatives in the Buddha Belt

Part 2

Bawi's Story

CONVERSION FROM CHRISTIAN TRADITION TO THE REAL JESUS

Bawi imagining himself as a Chin warrior

5

Awakening

Extraordinary sounds filled the sweaty room—a mishmash medley of speaking in tongues, shouting at demons, groaning, singing, wailing, and weeping. People outside the building saw demons fleeing. Inside the building, close to the middle of this now-famous Kalay Myo revival, stood an awkward, skinny teenager. That's me. On my left side a man passed out and was lying on the floor. On my right, a woman bumped into me, dancing with hands raised and eyes closed. My shoulders shook with uncontrollable sobs. The tears and sweat would not stop. Right there, in the middle of that musky, chaotic room, the Holy Spirit brought me alive on the inside. I would not be talking to you right now if not for that moment. Before then I was just a normal Chin kid—nominally Christian with selective historical amnesia. Consider the history that many of my people have forgotten.

STONE-FACED WARRIORS

We were slave-raiding savages, pillaging the dead and hunting for heads, until the British marched into Burma. Like it or not, the future had come. Our stone-faced warriors, once bold in battle, were no match for modern weapons and our battle swords soon stopped dripping with blood. We were also frightened spiritual polygamists: appeasing devils and bribing shamans until the Americans brought us Bibles. For centuries we had fearfully appeased demons with pig and goat blood. But our ritual sacrifices were no match for the cross of Christ, and soon our altars stopped dripping with blood too.

In those days my Chin people were an interesting contradiction: warrior kings in the visible realm and fear-fraught underlings in the invisible one. Today we are neither. By guns and the gospel, British generals and American missionaries, respectively, converted us on both accounts. In every direction, the blood has stopped flowing. Our people have changed so much in the last 250 years that our previous proud and shameful history hardly seems real. How different things are today than they were back then! Still, some things remain the same—the types of weapons and sacrifices are what's different.

It's about time I introduced myself. I'm Bawi, a peaceful Chin man who loves Jesus. I'm glad my people got the gospel all those years ago, but sometimes I imagine myself as an ancient Chin warrior. I don't want to scare people, but in my difficult years of sharing Jesus with a hostile Buddhist majority, I have often been scared myself. Maybe a huge headdress and a sharp spear would make me braver. Maybe they would at least make my oppressors think twice. Ha ha! Oh, my goodness.

EXPORTING CHRISTIANS

My Chin tribe comes from the northwestern mountains of Myanmar near the India border, where, as they say, "The only export is people." This short statement portrays two related truths: both the pathetic plight of the Chin State economy and our people's propensity for mass migration to the biggest and best places we can find. People joke that more of my people live in foreign countries than remain in the Chin Hills. This is probably an exaggeration ... or it may be true. I don't know exact numbers, but my people's reputation as relentless immigrants is definitely well-earned.

I have rarely met a Chin person who doesn't have at least one family member abroad. This is made possible, at least in part, by learning English in Bible school. Most of our Bible schools teach English as a subject, and many use it as the primary teaching medium. Students who learn English well gain opportunities to visit other countries for further study, Christian ministry, or other jobs. Some even go abroad as refugees, but that's a much longer road. Since so few jobs pay well in our country, family members working abroad are expected to send money home. This boosts the family's economic situation and their social status in the community. Every Chin family tries to send at least some of their children abroad, and Bible school is one of the surest routes. Religion, language, and economics are twisted together for my people like three strands of a rope. These three things have always been intertwined. But my people haven't always been Christian, the language hasn't always been English, and the economics haven't always been good.

Carson, East, Cope: the American missionaries who brought the gospel to the Chin Hills a century ago are still household names and heroes among my people. Unlike most other Myanmar ethnic groups, many Chin tribes accepted Jesus *en masse* and have idolized Americans ever since. The conversion was so thorough that certain subgroups of Chin are almost 100 percent Christian, at least in name. Many Chin say they are born Christian. I guess I was too. Then I met Jesus, and the trouble started. Ha ha! Amazing! I'm kind of joking but also kind of serious. My early life was like a fish following the current. After realizing the difference between knowing *about* God and knowing him *by experience*, I often found myself swimming against the stream, even in my own Christian community. In a way, that has brought me trouble. But the trouble has been worth it ... mostly, I think.

STEEPLES AND PAGODAS

In my hometown near the Chin foothills, every house boasts a sign over the front door: Evangel Pentecostal Fellowship, Global Harvest Assembly, Tidum Full Gospel, Emmanuel Baptist, or one of a thousand other church names. At first glance, a visitor might think every house in Kalay Myo is a church. But the signs are actually more like the blood of a Passover lamb—only to keep other churches away, rather than the death angel—which may even be worse! Oh my goodness! Sheep-stealing is such a popular pastime that each church requires its members to post the church name over their front doors. When everybody in town is Christian, I guess you do things like that. There's no way to grow one church without shrinking another—at least if you want to do it with Chin people, Chin language, and Chin customs, which we do.

Main Street in our dusty little town runs from one blistering end all the way to the other. Smaller neighborhood roads diverge on either side of Main Street like tree branches, but they don't go far. Most aren't paved either. If you want to go farther than your own neighborhood, you travel on Main Street. Just make sure not to go *too* far. About halfway down Main Street a line barricades both lanes of traffic, dividing the town in two. You can't miss this line and *don't* want to cross it; it separates the Chin Christians on one end of town from the Burmese Buddhists on the other. The line is not actually painted on the road—it's invisible—but even a first-time visitor would recognize the stark contrast between the sides.

On one side of the line, each neighborhood is crowned with steeples; on the other side, each hilltop with pagodas. On one side, church bells and congregational singing fill the air; on the other side, monastery bells and monk chants. On one side men wear pants and the walls wear Bible verses; on the other side, it's *longyis* (Burmese sarongs/man-skirts) and Buddha shelves. You get the picture. The differences go on and on. It's a clear division of "us" and "them." They speak their language; we speak ours. They buy and sell on their side; we do the same on ours. We're different from each other. We're separate. And we like it that way.

By now you're probably wondering: *With so many people who don't know Jesus right there on Main Street, why do churches have to steal each other's members to grow?* Good question. I guess it's because we don't want to cross the line. They worship statues, speak Burmese, and spit that despicable betel juice everywhere. The Burmese are infamous liars, cheats, and thieves. At least that's what most of us think. I used to think so too—until I met God and my thinking changed. Now I can see the sad irony of my people's blindness to the harvest field down the street, but many still cannot. I don't want to judge them. I just thank God he let me see.

Many of my Chin brothers and sisters have forgotten that we were no better than the Burmese before receiving the good news. We've also forgotten that the missionaries exchanged their refined homelands for our untamed jungles to make this possible. Many of them suffered and died prematurely from Burma's heartless tropical diseases. But the lack of medical care and human applause—even the stench of death—did not turn these unflinching missionaries away. They were crucified with Christ and willing to die for us to know him. Eventually, their perseverance paid off and our people welcomed the love of Christ. It was easy to believe Jesus laid his life down for us because we saw the missionaries laying their lives down too. Tears well up in my eyes as I think of all they went through to bring us the good news. Hallelujah!

But sadly, historic amnesia has turned many Chin people's focus inward. It's not that we have totally forgotten our past—we proudly boast in parts of it—but we have lost the memory of our hopelessness before the missionaries came. Ironically, we venerate the missionaries with our words, but denigrate them with our lives. We are content to fight over the ninety-nine sheep already in God's flock, rather than seeking to bring the lost ones back home. We compete among churches for the patronage of fellow Christians, rather than competing with the devil for those he binds in darkness. Many of my people need a reawakening—if not a rebirth. Here's how God did it for me.

ATTENTION PLEASE!

Back in that sweaty Kalay Myo revival meeting, I encountered the Holy Spirit and everything inside me changed. I sensed God telling me to stop seeking the temporary wealth of this world and seek the eternal wealth of his kingdom instead. I had wasted enough of my life pursuing the wrong thing! A season of deep sorrow and regret came over me like a thick cloud of depression. But the cloud lifted when I promised to serve God as an evangelist.

Life was different after experiencing the Holy Spirit. He gave me a deep, new desire for everyone to know Jesus. I couldn't stop weeping each day as I prayed for the Buddhists on the other side of Main Street. With no training or strategy, I started spontaneously crossing the invisible barricade and telling everyone I met about Jesus. How could I *not* tell people about him? He is *so* amazing! I couldn't rest until they knew him! This was all new for me. I had never told people about Jesus before, but now I could not stop. I no longer understood the majority of my people who were more concerned with money and church politics than taking the gospel to the other end of Main Street.

But as the Burmese saying goes, my passion to share the good news was "like a hay fire." It flared up quickly but didn't last long. Soon I was back to my old ways. The tears stopped flowing from my eyes, and the good news stopped flowing from my lips. I was dry—in every sense of the word. Once again, the pursuit of worldly wealth became more important to me than the interests of Jesus and his kingdom.

Then, one scorching summer day, I wearily strode down a sunbaked trail, forgetting to take water along. Dying for a drink and overwhelmed by the merciless heat, I began to feel weak and light-headed, like I might faint at any moment. Then, as I prepared to cross a little stream at the bottom of a hill, the lights went out. In my unconscious state, I saw faces with nooses around their necks orbiting in the sky like seats on a huge, invisible ferris wheel. Frightening flames flickered beneath them, threatening eternal doom. I could barely force myself to look! What could this mean? Then, I heard a voice: "You think this is hot? It's nothing compared to hell."

The next thing I knew, my face was pressed hard against the dirt trail near the little stream. Everything was sideways. I blinked a few times as consciousness returned. Then the meaning of the vision settled on me: It was a reminder of God's call on my life. I had broken my promise to forsake worldly pursuits and serve him by sharing the good news. Praise God for this vivid reminder—He is so gracious! He could have struck me with his shepherd's rod, but he kindly wrapped his staff around my neck and pulled me close instead. This was a clear warning to resume the gospel work he wanted me to do.

The fear of God welled up within me. God was not only a Good Shepherd, but also a consuming fire! I didn't want those faces to burn in hell like the vision had shown, and I didn't want to risk God's wrath on my life either. There was nothing else to do at that moment but pour my heart out to God. I dropped to my knees, confessed my sin, and begged for forgiveness. Our Heavenly Father ran to me with open arms, welcoming the prodigal son back home. Love replaced fear. Daily prayers and tears for the lost returned. My desire to share the good news returned too. After a few years of Bible School, I signed up to be a pioneer missionary on the opposite side of the country. I had no idea what was coming, but the plot was about to thicken with an army, a fire, and a taste of forbidden love.

GOD SHOT

God has given his people everything needed to live godly and useful lives, but he requires us to remember the gospel's cleansing work and supplement faith with virtue in order to experience its fullness.

> His divine power has given us everything required for life and godliness through the knowledge of him who called us by his own glory and goodness ...
>
> For this very reason, make every effort to supplement your faith with goodness, goodness with knowledge, knowledge with self-control, self-control with endurance, endurance with godliness, godliness with brotherly affection, and brotherly affection with love.

For if you possess these qualities in increasing measure, they will keep you from being useless or unfruitful in the knowledge of our Lord Jesus Christ. The person who lacks these things is blind and shortsighted and has forgotten the cleansing from his past sins. (2 Pet 1:3, 5–9)

PERSONAL REFLECTIONS

This is space to write personal discoveries, prayers, or anything else you find helpful. See this chapter's insights for mission in the back of the book or at jesusinthebuddhabelt.com.

6
Village Fire

Bump, curve, bump bounced the green Willy's Jeep up and around the tree-covered mountains on the mud-stone path to Banyan Ridge. Willy's weary engine revved and rocked along at the breakneck speed of seven miles per hour. Any faster on this road and either the Jeep, the passengers, or both, would break—or worse yet, permanently tumble off the cliff's unforgiving edge. The white-knuckled driver gripped the steering wheel like our lives depended on it—and they did. Tightly packed cargo and luggage filled the floor and roof spaces, and a handful of passengers bounced into each other in between. That's how I began the journey to my new mission field, with a full duffle bag, a fresh Bible degree, and a death grip on the back corner of the green Willy's Jeep.

I didn't know it yet, but that 1940s model Jeep would become an intimate friend over the years. I must have ridden it up and down the mountain several dozen times. Left behind by Allied forces after WWII, the US Army truck had long since been replaced with newer models in other countries. But it was still on the road in early twenty-first century Myanmar, partly because it was well-made and partly because cars were exorbitantly expensive in those days. Most of the cars were also old, the rugged ones particularly prized for their ability to manage the maintenance-free roads. I don't mean that the roads didn't *need* maintenance—just that they didn't get any. Ha ha! Amazing! Truthfully, the roads did get *some* maintenance, but it was slipshod, barely able to keep cars and passengers bouncing along on large rocks, mud ruts, and broken asphalt.

Our little Jeep, Willy, was a perfect match for the haggard roads. Willy and the roads were both old enough for retirement, but constant repairs kept them both bumping along mile by mile, trip by trip, year by year. Willy had seen better days, but could still handle the terrain as long as he maintained a tortoise pace and stopped a lot. And that's just what the driver did, pulling over at least once an hour to inspect Willy and give him a drink. Whether it was the Jeep or the driver that needed all those pit stops, I don't know—maybe they both did. All I know is we stopped *a lot* that day. Each time Willy's wheels started rolling again, I prayed for them to keep on rolling all the way to my new home before either the Jeep or the driver gave up and retired.

Poe, our *ka saya* (driver) also became an intimate friend through the years. Poe was as seasoned as Willy, except he wasn't loose and rattling all over. Despite his diminishing white hair, Poe still had a sharp jaw and keen eyes. Like a fighter pilot nestled in his cockpit, he peered at the road through black-rimmed glasses, ears sharply attuned to the Jeep. Each part of Poe's body played a role in getting us up the mountain. His left foot stomped the clutch pedal while his right hand jammed the wobbly gear shifter forward and back without thinking. Poe's left hand sturdily gripped the steering wheel, and his teeth safely sandwiched a smoldering cigarette. At times I doubted the Jeep's ability to get us up the mountain, but I never doubted Poe. I still don't know how he kept from biting that cigarette off over all the bumps.

While Willy, Poe, and the cigarette kept us bouncing up the mountain, I grinned like a child—full of faith, oblivious to the dangers ahead. My younger self saw no cause for worry as we rocked and curved into the unknown future. Like a child, I implicitly trusted that nothing was impossible for God and that he had a plan—which proved to be true—with many more surprising twists and turns than expected, of course. But that came later, along with sufficient grace. For the moment, my simple, child-like faith eased the butterflies in my stomach as we steadily climbed up and around the mud-stone path.

INITIAL IMPRESSIONS

I didn't know it would take eight hours to climb the last fifty-six miles to Banyan Ridge, but how long it took wasn't important to me; the important thing was just getting there. I prayed for our green Jeep along the way. I prayed for our driver. I prayed for my fellow passengers and the people of Banyan Ridge. And I prayed that God would use me to make a difference. As the Jeep bumped deeper into the jungle, I remembered a quote from Jesus: "If you have faith the size of a mustard seed, you will tell this mountain, 'Move from here to there,' and it will move." Before then, those words were little more than an artistic metaphor, but now, all of a sudden, they were concrete. In that moment, I knew the mountain I was bouncing up had to be moved, but it would only happen with the daring faith that Jesus taught.

Before I could finish that thought, our little Jeep crested the last steep peak. There we were, finally inhaling the crisp, cool air of Banyan Ridge. I could hardly believe it! But before I could fully absorb the moment, I was snapped to reality by a mountain proverb: "Close to see; far to walk," Poe said with a smile, pointing into the distance. You could see my new village just across the valley. Flower Village looked so close—and it *would be* close if you could drive there—but there was no road for cars. The footpath wasn't in a straight line either. A fellow passenger pointed it out in the distance. You could see it peeking through the trees in places, slowly turning back and forth through tea plantations, down one side and up the other. So began my Banyan Ridge acculturation course. I shouldered my duffle bag and started the long hike to Flower Village on foot.

What would the future hold in Flower Village? I had no idea, but I had time to think and pray it over as I put one foot in front of the other for the next few hours. Thanks to God's grace and a Christian acquaintance in the local government, I had been given official permission to enter the area as a Christian missionary. This was an obvious sign of God's favor. The Myanmar Buddhist majority does not smile on Christians trying to change their religion. Missionary work is strictly forbidden for foreigners. Myanmar people, on the other hand, are allowed to serve as pastors or ministers for existing Christians, but we can also get into trouble if we're perceived as trying to convert Buddhists to our religion. This is one reason we normally start new mission fields with some other type of work—education, healthcare, or business—something useful.

My government letter of approval, however, allowed me to skip all of that. Amazing! Instead of having to demonstrate other reasons for my presence in Banyan Ridge, I was able to openly explain my gospel motive. And no one could say anything about it—for a while at least. But that came later. For the moment, I enjoyed the perks of openly declaring my purpose.

THE PALAUNG

I didn't know much about Banyan Ridge before moving there, but I'm a certified expert now. Banyan Ridge is home to the richest Palaung tribe (or Ta'ang, as they call themselves). Their wealth comes from the highly coveted loose-leaf and pickled tea they produce. If you have ever tasted Banyan Ridge top-tier pickled tea, your mouth is probably watering right now. Or is it just me? If you haven't tasted it, I apologize. I can't describe the tender, juicy, bitter-sweet concoction nearly as well as your taste buds could, but I'll treat you when you visit my home. Ha ha! Back to the story. Tea has made the Palaung a household name in Myanmar and generated significant wealth for those who understand the business.

Banyan Ridge's relative prosperity and geographic isolation have helped insulate its Palaung population from most outside threats over the years (military, religious, business, etc.). Few people brave the arduous journey, and anyone who *does* manage to make it all the way up the winding, bumpy, mud-stone path falls under Palaung Army jurisdiction. A lot could be said about the Palaung Army, but for now, let's just say they cast a long shadow over the region and people fear them for good reason.

The Palaung origin story portrays the people of Banyan Ridge as the Palaung's eldest brother. This further entrenches their ethnic pride, giving them another reason to look down on their less educated, less wealthy tribesmen and those from other ethnicities.

All of these factors and more contribute to the Banyan Ridge Palaung's proud ethnic self-concept. They are wealthy, well-protected, and firstborn. They were also unified in those days, which bound them together in squashing divergent opinions. The village point of view was always right—new ideas were not welcome! Oh, and one more thing—they were staunchly and universally Theravada Buddhist—the strict, rule-following kind that would rather sink with the ship than accept help from a rescue boat. They were bound to Buddhism by uncountable links in the chain of tradition. Parents, village elders, teachers, and monks had built this chain from generation to generation as far back as anyone could remember. How could one insignificant person dare question it?

Do the confounding claims of a western-clad Jewish carpenter sound like a recipe for receptivity to new and different ideas? Looking back, I can see that the answer is emphatically *no*. In fact, if offered the same opportunity today, I'm not sure I'd go. Thankfully, it was my younger self bouncing around in the back of the Jeep that day. People warned me that the Palaung were *kaung ma-day* (hard-headed), even dangerous—and they were right. The Palaung are *kaung ma-day*. So were the people of Israel, so was the Apostle Paul, so was the Chin tribe a hundred years ago, and so was I before the Holy Spirit touched me in a Kalay Myo revival meeting. *Kaung ma-day* is just a way for God to show his glory. He turns the king's heart like a river of waters. He can move mountains with the minuscule faith of a mustard seed. "But will the Son of Man find faith when he comes to earth?" The hardness of Palaung heads did not concern me. God had sent me and he would take care of the rest. I was mostly sure of this most of the time, and also a little scared. Can I admit that?

WARMING UP

When I first moved to Flower Village in the 1990s, the average Myanmar family couldn't afford a car—many couldn't even afford a motorcycle. Every family could afford a bicycle, but those didn't fare well on steep mountain inclines. So this penniless, Bible school grad's primary means of transportation was a pair of flip-flops. And since everything in the mountains is "close to see, far to walk," I walked a lot. Walked again. Then walked some more—down one mountain and up another. Then back down the second, and back up the first. In the beginning, I was amazed at Palaung people's ability to climb steep mountains without breathing hard. Even children and grandmothers made it look easy. But day by day, all that walking turned me into a mountain goat. I could almost keep step with the locals.

All the walking developed another mountain-dwelling feature in me too—the appetite of a water buffalo. Thankfully, step by step, the people of Flower Village started warming up to me. Sometimes neighbors sent a few extra vegetables, some rice, or pickled tea to my hut. My stomach and my heart were both grateful for these gestures of kindness and trust. In the beginning, the villagers weren't that friendly—they were suspicious of my motives, and I don't blame them. Who knows what far-fetched fiction they had heard about me? But I taught their children, helped with their work, smiled a lot, and eventually earned their trust. That's when the sympathy food started coming. Sometimes they even invited me to sit and drink tea with them, that delicious Palaung tea!

LANGUAGE AND FRIENDS

Not only my legs and lungs, but also my tongue, needed lots of adapting to my new home. When I first moved to Flower Village, I only spoke two languages: Chin and Burmese. Neither of these was much help though. The Palaung didn't know the Chin language, and in the not-so-distant past, they reportedly killed people for speaking Burmese. Many Palaung people hated the Burmese and feared their militant schemes of forced subjugation. The *Tatmadaw's* village raiding, razing, and raping were prolific. Many from Palaung and other tribes fled to Thailand, and eventually to other countries to escape this violence from the Burmese-dominated military. Naturally, while all of this was happening, Burmese-speaking strangers were not welcome in Banyan Ridge. So my tongue had no choice—it had to speak Palaung.

Learning to speak Palaung was a marathon effort, but the benefits were worth it. Language learning demonstrated humility, helped me make friends, and gave the children something to laugh at. One time a village man taught me a new Palaung greeting. I proudly went around greeting everyone with perfect pronunciation and people thoroughly enjoyed it. Then someone had mercy and explained what the phrase meant: "I'm looking for a beautiful young lady to marry." Ha ha! Oh, my goodness!

I learned the first Palaung words by pointing at things. A willing villager would say a word and I would try my best to parrot it back. Children made the best teachers because they didn't tire of repeating themselves as quickly as adults. After hours and days, weeks and months of hard work and bloopers, I finally gained enough vocabulary to hold a basic adult conversation. The process endeared me to the villagers and helped get something I desperately needed—friends. With sympathy food, a growing grasp of the language, and a few friends, it felt like the mission was going in the right direction. But just as I was finally able to share the good news, the fledgling mission took a turn for the worse.

CONFLICT

The Palaung Literacy and Cultural Committee devised a system for writing their language and eagerly wanted everyone to learn it. I was eager to learn it too and signed up for the first available literacy class in Banyan Ridge. This was my big chance! How were these people going to understand the message of Jesus without the Bible in their language? I would have to translate the Bible, and the literacy class was the first step. The village leader gave me permission to attend, and I excitedly prepared for the session until a Palaung Army commander heard the news and forbade it. This started an inter-village feud.

Residents of Flower Village had grown to love me. But after the commander's prohibition, Big Village, our closest neighbor, fired up a campaign to force me out. Flower Village rallied to my defense. Then Big Village retaliated with economic sanctions. Nobody from Flower Village was allowed to sell goods in Big Village, and nobody from Big Village was allowed to sell in Flower Village. But even with this unneighborly bickering, Flower Village still refused to kick me out. Then Big Village took things a step further and barricaded the road so that no one from Flower Village could pass. Now residents of Flower Village had to take small footpaths through tea plantations to get to Banyan Ridge.

I was already traveling by footpath to avoid the stick-wielding hotheads who waited for me on the main road. Thankfully some friends from Flower Village warned me in time. "Surely this will all blow over soon," I thought. But it didn't. Then one day I started to question myself. "Why did I come to this place to begin with? Was it to bring good news or trouble?" I knew the answer: I came to bring peace, but I was causing strife instead. I came to share God's love, but I was evoking hatred. Whatever my motivation was, the only thing resulting now was trouble. Staying in the village felt like it was going against my greater purpose. Surely God didn't want this! Then, after much inner turmoil, many prayers, and countless tears, I decided to leave Flower Village and look for a rental house in Banyan Ridge.

WATER AND FIRE

It was a big transition from Flower Village to Banyan Ridge, but, thankfully, I had a few friends to help. They asked everyone in town about rental houses and found three. That's not very many houses, but I didn't need *many*—just one. And the third one was a perfect little place just off the main road.

My new wooden abode was simple: one downstairs room with a dirt floor and one upstairs room with a wooden floor. About 15 feet behind the house a mountain face shot straight up, leaving only enough room for an outhouse and small outdoor kitchen. I was thankful God had given this new house to restart in, but I grieved losing Flower Village too. It felt like the plug was pulled prematurely, just as all my hard work was starting to pay off. Now the nearly ripe fruit would rot on the vine, and I couldn't do anything about it. I wasn't ready to leave Flower Village, but

I had to, just like Jonah jumping off the boat to make the storm stop. That's how I felt, anyway. But the storm did not stop. I did not get swallowed by a large fish either. Amazing!

A few days later, while sitting on the wooden floor of my new home praying and pondering, I heard an intriguing conversation next door. "Most of the village has burned to the ground!" one neighbor excitedly reported to the other. "What village?" I wanted to ask, silently tip-toeing closer to the wooden wall between our houses. The neighbor continued, "They kicked the Christian teacher out, then this happened." *What?* Now I was really interested. I knew of no other Christian teacher in the area. They must have been talking about me. And the village that opposed me was Big Village... Surely it couldn't be true! But as the neighbors continued, I learned that it *was* true. Big Village had indeed burned to the ground. Oh my goodness! No one was hurt, but nearly every house in the village was lost. The devastation wouldn't be forgotten for a long time.

As you might imagine, everyone knows everything in a small community. News and gossip are as unstoppable as the Big Village fire was. For the past several weeks everyone in downtown Banyan Ridge had been talking about the feud between Big Village and Flower Village. This made the fire even bigger news. As the story spread, people naturally constructed cause-and-effect theories. For many village gossips, the reason was simple: the Christian God had taken revenge on Big Village for opposing his messenger. Amazing, isn't it? But I didn't have time to bask in the glory for long. I had a new mission to begin in Banyan Ridge and a new forbidden love to rescue.

GOD SHOT

God does not prevent his people from suffering, but he is present with them in the suffering and will deal out justice to their persecutors—either in the present or the future.

> *Therefore, we ourselves boast about you among God's churches—about your perseverance and faith in all the persecutions and afflictions that you are enduring. It is clear evidence of God's righteous judgment that you will be counted worthy of God's kingdom, for which you also are suffering, since it is just for God to repay with affliction those who afflict you and to give relief to you who are afflicted, along with us. This will take place at the revelation of the Lord Jesus from heaven with his powerful angels.*
>
> (2 Thess 1:4–9)

PERSONAL REFLECTIONS

This is space to write personal discoveries, prayers, or anything else you find helpful. See this chapter's insights for mission in the back of the book or at jesusinthebuddhabelt.com.

7
Love and Blindfolds

You'd probably laugh if I called an overgrown mountain village—with one narrow road, two restaurants, and zero electricity—a bustling metropolis. But that's exactly how Banyan Ridge felt compared to the much smaller Flower Village—and traffic started early. Fresh meat, exotic vegetables, and other delicacies from the big city lured morning market shoppers out of bed before the sun. And they proudly toted their newly purchased wares back past my front door before I could wipe the sleep crusties from my eyes. School children scurried by next—hundreds of them—playfully sporting green and white uniforms with multi-colored book bags haphazardly flung over one shoulder or the other. The children did this again each afternoon in the opposite direction, only with untucked shirts and empty lunch boxes. In between the school traffic, dozens of non-pupils passed my home—some on an errand, some for business, some just to visit a friend.

Then there was the non-human traffic—most often herds of cows or teams of tea-laden donkeys. They clopped past carelessly, steered by lazy swats from their herders' sticks. A few well-to-do cars and motorcycles buzzed by too, but not many. Only a handful of Banyan Ridge residents were wealthy enough to enjoy the luxury of motorized vehicles. Most of the human and non-human downtown traffic was on foot or hoof. This made me feel at home, since a pair of well-worn flip-flops was my only means of transportation too.

The daily parade past my new front door was more exciting than my quiet home in Flower Village, and the noise didn't bother me—except for the Chinese Engines. The smaller Chinese Engines were about the size of a traditional ox-drawn cart setup, with a little more cargo space in back. Larger Chinese Engines resembled crude pickup trucks, with minimal construction and no engine cover. Whether large or small, Chinese Engines are famous for their unmistakable clatter, each dawdling engine revolution exploding loudly enough to wake the village graveyard. Villagers loved the rugged and affordable Chinese Engines for their practicality. They could haul a load of tea, rice, or people up the bumpiest road on the mountain, tasks that otherwise required a team of hungry, messy donkeys. Townspeople, on the other hand, saw Chinese Engines as a noisy but necessary commodity.

Downtown Banyan Ridge buzzed and skipped from dawn to dusk, but the silent nights in between were almost as peaceful as Flower Village. After dark, the people, animals, and Chinese Engines returned home and closed the doors behind them, leaving only the moon and stars—oh, and chirping crickets. Candles and kerosene lanterns dimly lit the inside of Banyan Ridge homes until the children, parents, and grandparents drifted to sleep. No wonder most of us went to bed early. What else was there to do? Life was different before electricity—and in some ways probably better.

Each night before retiring, I opened the back door for one of my favorite parts of the evening. The walk to the wooden squatty potty was short but glorious—not because of the wood-framed hole in the ground, and certainly not because of the smell wafting out of it. No, I cherished my nightly trip to the toilet for the unpolluted view overhead—thousands of beaming stars silently telling their stories, praising their Maker, emanating peace. I wish you could have seen that brilliant sky before it disappeared. Banyan Ridge now has electricity. Power lines have brightened the streets and dimmed the stars. TVs and karaoke speakers have muted the cricket songs too. As I said, life was different before electricity—and in some ways probably better.

PROGRESS AND REGRESS

Life in downtown Banyan Ridge took some getting used to, but the adjustment was easier because I had already adjusted once in Flower Village. Flower Village ... I would be lying if I said I didn't miss it, but there was no going back now—only moving forward.

I began the new mission to Banyan Ridge with fresh resolve—putting my hand to the plow, continuing to learn the local language and culture, building mutual trust, sharing the good news, and eventually teaching a small handful of new believers. That's right—a few people in this isolated Buddhist stronghold actually believed the good news! I was excited to see the first fruit, but a new wave of opposition came with it—this time not directed at me, but at the fledgling converts.

Maung Khant was the first new Palaung believer in Banyan Ridge. He started well, ecstatic about finding Jesus and forgiveness. Maung Khant had said many prayers in his lifetime, but he had never known a God who heard and answered prayer like Jesus. He prayed often and found strength in his new faith. Maung Khant's life made a drastic change, and he was happy—despite being treated like a leper by his family and village—until the Palaung Army commander's death threat shook him to the core. Maung Khant was never the same after that. He became reclusive, withdrawing from everybody, even me. Life grew darker in isolation. Eventually, after no one had heard from him for several days, a neighbor peeked inside his silent house. There was Maung Khant, in his living room, with all the doors and windows shut, lifelessly dangling from a noose.

Maung Khant's suicide shook me to the core. I still feel confused when I think about it. But the effect of his death was different than I expected. Instead of scaring everyone away, Maung Khant's death somehow opened the way for more Banyan Ridge residents to follow Jesus. Soon, a young lady professed faith in Christ, then a few others. Some of these people professed faith for a while and then caved to social pressure and returned to Buddhism. Only a few remained. But what can I say? The pressure against them was stronger than anything most of us have ever faced. Growth was slow and required patience. One step forward, one step back. Two steps forward, one step back. Many days it hardly felt like progress at all. But month by month and year by year, a small number of Banyan Ridge residents—some Palaung and some from other tribes—persevered in faith and formed the first evangelical church in town.

FORBIDDEN LOVE

In addition to all the ups and downs of the new mission, I developed a personal problem—loneliness. I had moved to Banyan Ridge as a single man and quickly learned from personal experience that "it's not good for man to be alone." So I "chopped down two trees with one swing," by evangelizing my future wife. Ha ha! Oh my goodness! I actually did that.

I knew Sky was forbidden fruit, but she was fun-loving and spunky, with a quick wit—and that smile! Every week I went from house to house sharing the good news, but my feet knew the way to her house better than the others. I shared the gospel and got to know her more with each visit. You're probably thinking, "Come on, Bawi! Don't you know missionary dating is a bad idea?" I *did* know it was a bad idea—and I don't recommend it to others—but who else was I going to marry out there? There weren't any Christians! Dating evangelism was the only escape I could see from loneliness. Did I say I don't recommend it to others?

I didn't share the gospel with Sky *only* so I could marry her; I shared the gospel with everyone who would listen—that's why I moved to Banyan Ridge in the first place. But the more I got to know Sky, the more attractive she became. This was an extra incentive for sharing the gospel. But the odds of Sky walking down the aisle with me and Jesus still weren't good. Problem one: Palaung people are only supposed to marry Palaung people—even the particular clan is spelled out by their tradition. Marriage to someone from the wrong clan—much less the entirely wrong ethnic group—is strictly off-limits. But this was the least of our troubles. Problem two was much bigger: Sky was forbidden from marrying someone from a different religion. Her parents and village leaders were afraid she would become a Christian if she married one. We were stuck right there, strictly forbidden from the two things my heart was set on: Sky becoming a Christian and her marrying a Christian—namely, me.

DECISION

In addition to family and village pressure, Sky also had a significant obstacle of her own to overcome—a neighboring Christian village. Yep. Ironically, a Christian village was one of Sky's biggest barriers to following Jesus. The gospel sounded great to Sky: God forgives you, makes you new, and takes you to be with him forever outside of suffering! But if all that was true, why did the neighboring Kachin Christian village abuse alcohol, beat their wives, and gossip worse than Buddhists? Sadly, Sky saw more bad habits in the Kachin Christians than in her Palaung neighbors.

It took a lot of explaining, thinking, and praying for Sky to overcome the stumbling block of these so-called Christians. At times, I didn't think she was going to make it, but Sky eventually decided to follow Jesus. Amazing! By God's grace, I was able to "chop down two trees with one swing," gaining both a new sister in Christ and a new partner for life. My loneliness was finally over!

Many questioned Sky's motive for following Jesus. Was it out of love for Jesus or Bawi? I thought about that too. Maybe love for Jesus *and* love for Bawi factored into her decision. It's hard to say. Either way, Sky's conversion to Christ did come *before* our engagement and marriage—and she did choose to follow Jesus despite fierce opposition from her family and village community. It looked like Jesus and I had both chosen Sky, and she had chosen both of us. I didn't understand it all. I just accepted her profession of faith sincerely—and celebrated with double joy. Sky was baptized before our marriage, and over the years her faith has often shone brighter than my own, inspiring me and many others.

DREAM

One night shortly after our marriage, Sky received a message in a dream. A voice called to her from outside the house: "Daughter, do you want to see your Savior?" Still a recent convert from Buddhism, Sky stepped through the doorway, expecting to see the

Lord Buddha. Instead, she was surprised by a white-robed man with pointy shoes, who she immediately recognized as the Lord Jesus. She jostled me awake and explained. What did the dream mean? We took it as a confirmation that Jesus was her Savior—not the statues she grew up worshipping. Sky found great comfort in that dream and has faithfully followed Jesus ever since.

She really is, as the Scriptures say, "a suitable helper" to me—a strong support in so many ways. Without Sky, I would never have lasted so long in the chilly mountains of Banyan Ridge. I definitely wouldn't have these three beautiful children and the pure joy they bring. I'd probably be a lot skinnier too. Ha ha! Sky is a great cook, and over the years it has caught up with my gut a little. But that's okay. It's good to have a big belly where I live. It lets people know you provide well for your family, and your wife puts plenty of delicious food on the table. I guess my expanded gut is another piece of evidence that it's not good for man to be alone—at least in my case. Sky and I would both tell you that marriage hasn't always been easy, but we work at it and mostly make a pretty good team. She cooks and I eat.

FRUIT

I've been in the mountains of Banyan Ridge for over twenty years now. Sometimes I can't help but consider the fruit of my labor. It's hard to reduce two decades into two sentences and act like you're measuring something, but here goes: I've got a beautiful Christian wife, three great kids, and a small church that I shepherd. A few Palaung people have come to faith. Others have come to faith from other ethnic groups. Some Christians have also moved to town and joined our little group along the way. It's a motley crew, and imperfect, but our Banyan Ridge church is alive and shining in the darkness.

I've sent a few promising converts to Bible school, hoping they would return to lead the church, but none of them have panned out. They went to school with a zeal to teach their people about Christ's love, but ended up finding better things to do. I guess a taste of the big city and a wider path of opportunity changed their perspective. So I'm still leading the church. We're still plodding along while my hairline is receding.

If you zoom out on the past two decades, the gospel work in Banyan Ridge might look like a tortoise, slowly inching toward an invisible finish line, just past the edge of the horizon. When I first packed my duffle bag and headed to these mountains, I never imagined being a tortoise—there is too much ground to cover—too many people that need the good news. No, I wanted to run at a hare's pace! I wanted to see *hordes* of people rescued from the devil's grip and brought into God's family, shaking the waters of baptism—early and often! Isn't that a much better way for the good news to spread? I wanted to return home with powerful stories of God's work that would give him glory and inspire others to missionary service.

None of those dreams have completely come true. But I *do* see God's hand in my work. I *do* feel his blessing with me—even if it's only one step forward, one step back. Two steps forward, one step back—a slow, slogging tortoise pace with God.

ANOTHER FIRE

I told you about a fire that flattened Big Village after they forced me out almost two decades ago. More recently there was another fire. This one devoured most of downtown Banyan Ridge, which by this time had become a provincial capital. The fire started in a home near the center of town. Authorities guessed that a poorly wired electrical box short-circuited and burst into flames. The fire spread to the neighboring homes on either side, gaining speed in both directions.

At the time, nearly every house in Banyan Ridge was built of wood, each tightly crammed against the other, with many even sharing exterior walls. The fire raged wildly, spreading from one house to the next in a matter of minutes—sometimes only seconds. It blew across the narrow street and back again, devouring most of the city in less than an hour.

From a distance, the town looked like a giant bonfire. The fire department made a valiant effort, but their equipment looked like toy water guns meaninglessly spitting on the roaring blaze. All the fire department could do was snuff out the smolders once the flames had eaten their fill.

"How'd the fire stop?" you ask. That's the part I want to tell you. The fire kept raging because the wooden houses were crammed against each other with no space in between. Only a separation between the houses could stop the fire, but there *was* no separation—until one man offered to sacrifice his home. As the fire moved down the street, devouring one house after another, this man preemptively leveled his house, creating a gap too wide for the fire to cross. The fire department shot every ounce of water they could on the remaining rubble, and the fire finally sizzled to a halt. The houses on the other side were saved. Granted, the house that was destroyed would have been consumed by fire anyway, but tearing it down was a deliberate sacrifice of one for the benefit of many others. Interestingly, no one else in Banyan Ridge thought to do this—just one man—and he happens to be a Christian. What do you think of that?

MISSING THE PICTURE

Doesn't this Christian man voluntarily destroying his house to save the others beautifully depict the love of Christ? It's clear to me, but, sadly, I don't think anybody else in town saw the connection—even when I explained it—except for the handful of Christians. How incapable we are of seeing until Christ removes the blindfold! The people of Banyan Ridge are held captive in the domain of darkness. They can't get out by their own will or missionary persuasion. We can tell people about the light—we must!—but we can't make them see it; only God can. Maybe that's why Adoniram Judson, the great pioneer missionary to Burma, often prayed, "Lord, give them light!" Exactly how it all works is a mystery to me, but I have come to believe two things deeply over the past two decades in Banyan Ridge: 1) God has given us an essential part in fulfilling his mission—may he grant us grace and power to do it faithfully, and 2) there is a part of God's mission that only he can do.

After all the ways God has shown himself in Banyan Ridge, I often wonder why people still have not turned to him in significant numbers. I'm not saying my part has been perfect—it certainly hasn't. But I have seen enough blindness and lethargy to know that something else is needed too. I think what the people of Banyan Ridge need most is for God to open their blind eyes. God must remove the blindfold if they are going to see. This realization has driven me to rely less on other missionary efforts and give myself more fully to the most important missionary task of all, getting on my knees in prayer.

I am convinced that desperate prayer is the only way God's kingdom will move forward in Banyan Ridge. I can't help but wonder what would happen if enough of us started approaching this noble knee work as the crucial part of God's mission that it is. When we seriously hit our knees on behalf of the lost, will God not rend the heavens and come down? Can there still be a great movement of Palaung people to Christ in Banyan Ridge? I don't understand the deep mystery of God's will, but at least for my part, I'm not ready to let go of that hope just yet. And I wonder if you, my new friend, might consider joining me in this noble knee work, begging God for his kingdom to come and his will to be done here on earth, just like it is in heaven.

GOD SHOT

God has designed the Great Commission as a partnership between him and his people. We pray, plant the gospel seed, and water it—but God makes things grow. He performs the miracle of conversion and enables the spiritual growth that follows, not us.

> *What then is Apollos? What is Paul? They are servants through whom you believed, and each has the role the Lord has given. I planted, Apollos watered, but God gave the growth. So, then, neither the one who plants nor the one who waters is anything, but only God who gives the growth.*
>
> (1 Cor 3:5–7)

PERSONAL REFLECTIONS

This is space to write personal discoveries, prayers, or anything else you find helpful. See this chapter's insights for mission in the back of the book or at jesusinthebuddhabelt.com.

8

Going Deeper: Becoming Like a Buddhist (to Win Some to Jesus)

The sun shone high in a cloudless sky on our second day hiking to Banyan Ridge. "Take off your shoes and follow me," I said to the exhausted group of backpackers. We had already been climbing steep trails for several hours and most of the group hadn't slept well on the village floor the night before. The shaded stairway at the bottom of our next rest stop was a welcome sight. The relieved Europeans dropped their jumbo backpacks and untied their hiking boots. "Ready to visit the monastery?" I asked, as the last one pulled off his socks. "I'm ready for you to carry me up those stairs," joked the energetic group leader. I laughed and pretended to lift him by one leg before starting the barefoot climb up the cool concrete steps.

The weary trekkers bounced up behind me, renewed by the prospect of rest and scenic views at the top. "Remember what I told you earlier," I reminded them as we gathered in front of the monastery's large wooden doors. They nodded as we crossed the worn wooden threshold to meet the senior monk. "*Mingalaba*, Pone Pone," I said with a smile. "*Mingalaba* to all of you, and welcome," he replied, happily returning my greeting. "How can I help you?"

"This group of tourists wants to meet you and see the monastery," I explained. "Then, please, take a seat," he kindly offered. By now this was a familiar routine for both of us. I often guided trekkers through the area, and most of them liked stopping here for tea and conversation. I think the monk enjoyed our visits too—he sure did ask a lot of questions anyway.

Gilded Buddha statues, murals of his past lives, rugged architecture, and long lists of donors—the tourist group's wide eyes scanned the monastery while I exchanged pleasantries with the monk. Their eyes stopped wandering when I sat down. I had previously instructed the group to copy my every move once inside the monastery. I try to help my guests avoid offending anyone, but especially monks, the revered gods of Buddhism. Tourists usually don't intend to offend the local people, but without some guidance, they often do so by mistake. Myanmar culture is different from Western countries—sometimes totally opposite. It's hard to explain every cultural nuance, so I usually just tell the tourists to copy me. So far this group was doing okay.

The trekkers' eyes were glued to me as I accepted the monk's invitation to sit. I chose the lower level of the floor, turned my body and knees toward the monk, and pointed my feet behind me—away from the monk and Buddha statues. The Europeans carefully did the same. Every move inside the monastery must communicate respect to the monk and Buddha statues. This was especially important for us since we were already breaking the normal pattern of monastery interaction. Everyone else who walked through the doors greeted the monk with worship: calling him "god" and bowing their heads to the ground three times at his feet. Thankfully, the monk does not expect worship from me, since I visit often and he knows I'm a Christian. But if I didn't show him kindness and respect, we wouldn't have a cordial relationship, and he wouldn't welcome these tour groups. He definitely wouldn't listen to the important message I have to tell him. As the Burmese proverb says: "Friendly with the person; friendly with the teaching."

The monk disappeared and returned with a thermos of tea, six tiny porcelain cups, and a jar of *tanyat* (a locally produced palm sugar treat). He slowly filled each cup with steaming tea and handed them to me one by one. I passed each one to the guest next to me, and he did the same until everyone had a cup. We all enjoyed our first steaming sip of Palaung tea, while the tourists guessed what the mysterious brown balls of *tanyat* might be. "Thank you, Pone Pone," I said with a smile.

Then turning toward the trekkers, I set up the conversation: "Is there anything you would like to ask the monk?" And with that, they were off. The Europeans asked about the statues and murals in the monastery, the principles of Buddhism, the tea, *tanyat*, and whatever else came to mind. The monk proudly answered their questions, then volleyed back a few of his own. "How does the Leaning Tower of Pisa work? What's the average salary in Europe? Are your monks allowed to marry?" The monk had all kinds of questions about other countries, and he loved to compare various travelers' answers.

Sometimes these exchanges lasted only a few minutes, other times they lasted for hours. This one lasted two pots of tea and half a jar of *tanyat*—two good indicators of Banyan Ridge Mountain Time. We had a good conversation with the monk that day. And even though the tourists weren't practicing Christians, I got to weave a few additional threads into my ongoing Jesus conversation with the monk. After all these years, navigating monk conversations has become simple. But I remember a time when it wasn't. In the early days, my Banyan Ridge IQ wasn't much better than the foreign groups I now lead on hikes.

PAUL'S STRATEGY

This bright-eyed kid knew lots of things when I first showed up in Banyan Ridge—at least I thought I did. You know: the names of Israel's minor prophets, the history of Christian mission to my Chin people, the doctrinal distinctions of major Christian denominations, how to defend the faith, etc. I knew a lot from my Christian upbringing on the other side of the country, where the temperature was high, the land was flat, and the truth was printed in black and white. Bible School taught me more. But after all those lessons, I still knew little about mountain life and even less about Buddhism.

Even though Myanmar is a majority Buddhist country, my tribe is nearly all Christian. We grew up trying not to intermingle with people who didn't believe like us. That's how I made it to adulthood without understanding the people down the street. I had lots of new skills to learn those first years in Banyan Ridge:

how to stay warm in the chilly mountains, how to get water home from the stream, how to pick and sort tea, and loads of other mountaineering skills. But one of the biggest things I had to learn in Banyan Ridge was how to meaningfully interact with my Buddhist neighbors.

The Apostle Paul said:

> To the Jews I became like a Jew, *to win Jews;*
>
> to those under the law, like one under the law ... *to win those under the law.*
>
> To those who are without the law, like one without the law ... *to win those without the law.*
>
> To the weak I became weak, *in order to win the weak.*
>
> I have become all things to all people, *so that I may by every possible means save some.* Now I do all this because of the gospel, so that I may share in the blessings.
>
> (1 Cor 9:20–23, emphasis added)

If Paul became all those different things to all those different people *in order to win them to Jesus*, how should I approach the Banyan Ridge Buddhists? It seemed like Paul was saying, "You've got to become like the people—understand them and meaningfully relate to them—if you want them to know Jesus." This stirred a question that went against all my hometown upbringing—should I "become like a Buddhist" to win Buddhists to Jesus? Asking this question felt strange, but I needed to answer it correctly if I hoped to lead the Banyan Ridge people to God.

I struggled, prayed, and thought it over before finally deciding to imitate this part of Paul's strategy. I started studying Buddhism—not in order to become a Buddhist—but in order to understand them better, so that I could communicate with them better. How could I effectively point people to Jesus without understanding them? What beliefs and practices were keeping them *from* Jesus? And might any of their beliefs and practices help point them *to* Jesus? During this period of studying Buddhism, my Christian beliefs and practices didn't change. Instead, they were strengthened in contrast with the new things I learned.

LEARNING FROM MONKS

I found out everyone had something to teach me once I started asking questions. The local villagers taught me mountain life and folk Buddhist culture. But most of the villagers didn't know proper Buddhist teaching. For that, I turned to the monks.

By this point, the monastery wasn't new to me. I had already been attending village events there—a festival, funeral, political gathering, or civic meeting—something was always going on. I knew the monks from a distance. We just didn't have a relationship, and I didn't know how to start one either. The first thing every Buddhist does in the presence of a monk is bow at their feet three times, addressing them as god. There were lots of things I felt okay doing at the monastery—listening to the preaching, helping with cooking, sweeping, setting up for events—all those were fine. But I could not bow down to the monk and call him god. No, I could never do that! I felt stuck at this very first stage of interaction.

It's hard to understand how central the monastery is to village life until you live there. It's not only a religious center, but a cultural hub as well. The monastery hosts most of the community's monthly festivals and all of the funerals. Large wedding parties often cook and host receptions there (no one else has large enough pots). The monks live at the monastery and provide other valuable services as well: teaching children, explaining the path to *nirvana*, giving life to Buddha statues, and blessing and protecting new homes from spirits. The monks are the most educated people in the village. This, along with their god-like status, helps them wield great power over the simple-minded villagers. With few exceptions, they reign as sovereign kings. I had already met the monk-kings and exchanged cordial pleasantries on my frequent trips to the monastery, but discussing matters of religion with them was another thing entirely. Still, it was time to try.

Beyond the whole "I'm not bowing down and calling you god" thing, there are lots of other reasons it's intimidating to talk to monks. For starters, you have to learn a new vocabulary just to address them. For example: Burmese language uses special pronouns for everybody. The pronouns for "you" and "me" are different if you're talking to someone your little brother's age, your same age, a few years older, fifteen years older, or thirty years older than you. The pronouns also change based on gender and social status. Monks have a different class of pronouns too—along with a slew of special verbs. Using these terms—especially the pronouns—forces you to call the monks god and yourself their disciple. Telling a monk, "I brought you some rice," for example, forces you to say the equivalent of, "Lord god, your disciple has brought you an offering of holy rice."

Could I use these terms and remain faithful to my Lord? Could I avoid them without offending the monks? I struggled for months before finding a work-around that both the monks and I felt comfortable with. I use the special verbs for monks, but I do not use the pronouns which call them god. My most frequently used term is *Pone Pone*. In Burmese, monks are called *Pone Gyi*, literally meaning "big glory." *Pone Pone* is a friendly and respectful variation of this. The term *Pone Pone* has helped me build good relationships with monks who are willing to try.

It's worth pointing out that not all monks are equally approachable: some are humble and open, but others are proud and inflexible. Thankfully, the head monk in my village was a friendly, civic personality as well as a religious leader. He graciously forgave many mistakes as I learned how to talk to him. Conversations with monks and the books they recommended deepened my understanding of the Buddhist mind: the *Four Noble Truths*, the *Noble Eightfold Path*, the *Law of Karma*, the *Cycle of Samsara*, the *Signs of Suffering*, the *Jataka Tales*, etc.

Buddhist concepts became less foreign with each lesson and page. Surprisingly, I discovered lots of Buddhist teaching that lined up with the Bible. Lots of it contradicted the Bible too—especially concerning salvation. But whether similar or different, all the Buddhist teachings I learned helped me understand my neighbors better—what's important to them, what barriers are keeping them from Jesus, and what bridges from Buddhism might actually point them to Jesus. All of this has led to great conversations about the good news.

GENERAL AUNG SAN

One of the deepest concepts ingrained in the Buddhist mind is that there's no one to save you—everything hinges on your own ability to follow the teachings. This is directly opposed to the good news of Jesus, which begins with the principle of human inability. Jesus teaches that people can never do enough good deeds; we can only be saved by faith in what he has done for us. Any Buddhist who genuinely considers the way of salvation will have to grapple with these contradictory claims. Their question is: "How can what Jesus did be applied to me?" The Buddhist teaching of *karma* has hardwired its followers against the concept of salvation, but we can help Buddhists understand salvation with analogies from their daily lives. These analogies, which they already know, can become bridges to Jesus, whom they don't yet know. This approach won't automatically turn Buddhists to Jesus, but it can remove some of the barriers in their way—becoming "all things to all people," so we might "by every possible means save some."

I often use the national hero General Aung San to explain how Jesus's death can set us all free. Aung San was a key figure in the Burmese struggle for independence. There's not a person in Myanmar who doesn't know his name. His picture is plastered in homes, businesses, and Facebook profiles across the country. His daughter, Aung San Suu Kyi, continues his legacy as a national hero and icon for freedom fighters today. During World War II, General Aung San joined Japanese forces to drive British colonists out of Burma. After suffering the harshness of Japanese rule, Aung San changed his mind and rejoined the British to force the Japanese back out of the country.

After WWII, General Aung San helped negotiate Burma's independence from the British. He's also famous for rallying many of the country's ethnic minorities to join the newly formed federal state union. The young country's prospects were bright when Aung San's political party won an overwhelming majority in the April 1947 general election. Then, three months later, a group of military-clad assassins stormed the Secretariat Building in Rangoon (Yangon), gunning down Aung San and eight of his cabinet members. This was a tragic day in Burmese history. Aung San had negotiated and fought for Burmese independence, and now he died for it. But his dream of freedom did not die with him— it became a reality for the whole country the following January when the last British soldiers departed Burma.

Today General Aung San is a universal icon of freedom in Myanmar. Each year the national holidays of Union Day and Martyrs' Day remind us of the ultimate price he paid to set us free. Though many others were involved in the struggle as well, Aung San is the most notable. We know him as the one who gave his life for our freedom. Every citizen of British Burma did not struggle and die for independence like General Aung San, but every citizen experienced the freedom his sacrifice gained. The people of Burma no longer needed to fight for freedom; all we had to do was receive the victory someone else had already won for us.

That's like the good news of Jesus. We were all held captive, oppressed by sin and the devil. As badly as we wanted to, we couldn't escape in our own strength—our enemy was too strong. Then Jesus came announcing "freedom to the captives ... [and] the oppressed" (Luke 4:18). But this freedom was not easily gained. Jesus paid the ultimate price to secure our freedom with his death on the cross. In Jesus's death on the cross, he settled all of humanity's sin debt. Then he did something even more incredible—rose from the dead! By Jesus's sinless life, sacrificial death, and victorious resurrection, he has conquered sin, death, and the devil for all humanity! There is no more battle to fight! Our freedom has already been won! Only those who reject Jesus's victory on their behalf remain enslaved in the hopeless cycle of *karma*, sin, and suffering. "Christ has liberated us to be free" (Gal 5:1). All we have to do is embrace him with repentance and faith.

BACK TO THE MONASTERY

After exhausting all questions in both directions, the trekkers thanked the monk for his kindness and placed their teacups back on the tray next to mine. "Pone Pone," I said softly in Burmese, as we walked to the door, "You have learned much about Jesus, haven't you?" He smiled and silently nodded. I looked into his eyes, past the monk exterior to his real inner self, and lovingly pressed in a way that only deep relationships can: "When will you come to him as Lord?" He stopped walking and looked into the distance for a thoughtful moment. Then he grabbed my hand and silently walked me to the top of the stairway where the tourists were putting on their shoes. "Go slowly, friends," he told them, with classic Palaung etiquette. Then turning toward me, he said with a smile, "Please come again, friend. You are always welcome. I will think about your question."

GOD SHOT

God is a relational being. He relates to himself within the Trinity and invites us to a restored relationship with him through the gospel. God extends this invitation, at least in part, through human relationships.

> *Everything is from God, who has reconciled us to himself through Christ and has given us the ministry of reconciliation. That is, in Christ, God was reconciling the world to himself, not counting their trespasses against them, and he has committed the message of reconciliation to us. Therefore, we are ambassadors for Christ, since God is making his appeal through us. We plead on Christ's behalf, "Be reconciled to God."*
>
> (2 Cor 5:18–20)

PERSONAL REFLECTIONS

This is space to write personal discoveries, prayers, or anything else you find helpful. See this chapter's insights for mission in the back of the book or at jesusinthebuddhabelt.com.

DISCUSSION AND PRAYER GUIDE

This was the final chapter in Bawi's story. See the Discussion and Prayer Guide in the back of this book for deeper personal or group reflection or scan the QR code for an online version.

jesusinthebuddhabelt.com
Also scan this QR code to:

SHARE your thoughts or ask a question

EXPLORE the topics of this book further with free articles, photos, videos, and recipes

CONNECT with ongoing mission initiatives in the Buddha Belt

Part 3
Lin's Story

THE BRIGHT AND DARK SIDE OF CHRISTIAN MISSION IN MYANMAR

Lin in Anya, before moving to the big city

9
Adoption

Thud! Thud! Thud! I still remember the sound of my mother pounding fish paste in the outdoor kitchen her small, sturdy frame squatting over the mortar and pestle, pausing now and then to wipe the sweat from her forehead. Finally, *A-may* (the Burmese word for mother) dumped the mass of salt and smashed fish into a clay bowl and set it in the sun to ferment. Then she walked back under the lean-to and started cooking dinner. A few months later, our favorite condiment was crawling with maggots and ready to enjoy. You can tell *nga-pi* is ready by its unmistakable smell. That is where your love—or hate—relationship with *nga-pi* starts. As soon as your nose detects it, your feet want to run in one of two directions. Singaporeans despise the smell so much that they have banned it from cooking. My people, on the other hand, can hardly eat rice without it. My mouth is watering as I describe it now. It is funny how people's mouths can be so different—one is salivating while another is gagging over the same thing.

    Here is another way our mouths differ. How do people greet each other where you are from? Probably something nice like, "Hello, good morning." Where I am from, people curse you ten times before saying hello—and that is on a good day. Our mouths are quite different are they not? Welcome to Anya, a place with hot weather and hot tempers, where fast, foul talk makes sailors blush. The only thing more foul than an Anya mouth is the *nga-pi* we put into our mouths. At least some people think *nga-pi* is foul. In Anya, we like it almost as much as our curse words.

    Why am I beginning with profanity and fermented fish? To show that we are different—me and you, my hometown and yours, my people and yours. Of course, we are the same in many ways too, but there are real differences. Sometimes it is hard to understand the differences until you get to know a person and hear their story—walk a mile in their flip-flops. Then things start to make more sense, like why I nearly hacked Su Su's brothers to death with a machete—even after knowing Jesus. I am not saying it was the right thing to do, just that where I come from it is not unusual.

ANYA

My name is Lin. I grew up in a small Burmese village with *A-may* and two sisters. My dad got sick when I was a kid and never recovered. People warned us not to take him to the hospital or he would die. We took him anyway, and he did. I do not know if the hospital is to blame or not, but a lot of people do die there. Growing up without a father left a hole in me that is still there. But thank God for an amazing mother, who did her best to make up for it. *A-may* had a rough sunbaked exterior, but her heart was butter-soft toward her children—especially after she came to know Jesus.

The log frame, bamboo walls, and thatch roof of our handmade bungalow inconspicuously blended into the desert plain of middle Myanmar, where pure Burmese villages still exist untainted by other races. Unlike big cities and ethnic areas, nobody lives in Anya but the Burmese. And no language is spoken but Burmese. As you might imagine, there is not much diversity of opinion in a place like that. Anya people are unapologetically attached to our long-held ways of doing things. We are proud to be Burmese—the largest ethnic group in the country, descendants of mighty kings, purveyors of Burmese language and culture to Myanmar's 134 smaller tribes.

I do not know why the original settlers chose to make Anya their home. The heat is blistering, it does not rain much, and the sand and wind make it impossible to keep things clean. Do not try growing anything unless your village happens to be along the river. Otherwise, your thirsty crops will scorch in the desert. Despite its harsh climate, there is a happy place in Anya—the front porch in the evening. This brief moment of respite from the sun is a welcome ending to a hot day. Friends and neighbors grab a bottle of *tan-yi* (locally produced palm sugar wine), gather on the porch, and aimlessly shoot air guns (a local saying for "shooting the breeze") before turning in for the night.

RACISM AND WAR

The friends we shoot air guns with on the porch are all Burmese. We are more likely to shoot real guns with other tribes. It is not that friendships in our country never cross ethnic lines—they do, especially among certain groups—but each tribe's deeply ingrained racism and the ongoing military conflict do not make it easy. Most of the ethnic minority groups hated the Burmese back then, at least where the *Tatmadaw* (Burmese-dominated military) was active. I learned all this once leaving home and getting to know people from ethnic minority groups. Anya wasn't ethnically diverse, so we filled in the blank with stereotypes.

Burmese make up 60 percent of Myanmar's population and we are everywhere. We hold most of the powerful positions in government, schools, and the *Tatmadaw*. A lot of minority people are uneducated hill tribes who cannot speak our language correctly—at least that is what I used to think before meeting Jesus. Living among ethnic minorities changed my perspective too, but we will save that for later.

The hatred among tribes in our country is nothing new. It has deep roots in our ancient history and has been exacerbated in new ways in the two hundred years since British colonization. Various ethnic armies have been fighting the *Tatmadaw* since 1948. This is the longest-standing civil war in the world, and the battle lines are drawn by race and religion. Burmese people make up most of the *Tatmadaw* fighting force, but you do not have to be Burmese to enlist. You do have to be Buddhist if you want to get promoted though. Christians and others from non-Buddhist religions can hardly advance past the military's lower ranks. Ethnic armies also tend to form along racial and religious lines. The Karen, for instance, have divided into separate Buddhist and Christian fighting forces. The Kachin army is all Christian. The Palaung is Buddhist, and so on. Everywhere you look, race and religion are dividing people.

With all these different fighting forces, who is right and who is wrong? Growing up in Anya, I would have answered one way. While living among ethnic minority groups, I may have answered differently. Since the 2021 coup, I have seen the dark side of the *Tatmadaw* in new ways, but I also do not know if the other armies will turn out any better. I just know they are all still shooting, and I see no end in sight. Peace talks bear no fruit. The people at the table do not trust each other—and why should they? They sign ceasefire agreements but do not stop shooting. Racial and religious hatred is the air we breathe. No amount of talking or signatures can change that. Only walking among the minorities and coming to know Jesus has changed it for me. Without many others experiencing this, I see no peaceful way forward.

I have to admit, though, that race relations surprisingly improved after the 2021 coup. Since then, the *Tatmadaw* has been fighting everyone, regardless of ethnicity—even our own Burmese people. In the past, the *Tatmadaw's* raping, razing, and shooting were confined to the ethnic minorities. But the Burmese people are no longer exempt. We are also being attacked and have formed inter-ethnic People's Defense Forces (PDFs) all over the country. At the moment, the various ethnic groups of Myanmar are being brought together by a common enemy. We will see how this develops after the revolution.

VILLAGE HEARSAY

When I was growing up, nobody in the village knew about Jesus. We knew there was a Christian religion that worshipped Jesus, but that was a *foreign* religion for *foreign* people. Whites from other countries worshipped Jesus, along with some of the hill tribes that they converted. However, the hill tribes did not know any better—Buddhists do. We have a systematic religion that our mothers, fathers, teachers, and monks have faithfully passed down to us for generations. The hill tribes did not have a proper religion, leaving them with an empty cup for Christianity to fill. Of course, people with an empty cup are looking for something to fill it. Buddhists' cup, on the other hand, is already full. And since all Burmese are Buddhist, not many have converted to Christianity. It took over six years for Adoniram Judson to baptize the first Burmese convert, and over 200 years later less than 1 percent have become Christian.

As a kid, I also heard that Christians buy converts. Using gifts and money to manipulate religious convictions disgusted us. People will do just about anything to get money—but money does not change who they are inside. Thankfully, not many Burmese were duped by this religious profiteering, only a few short-sighted sellouts. The Christians might have more money than us, but that did not mean their religion was better.

I grew up hearing other rumors about Christians too. They initiate converts by dunking their heads underwater until they see Jesus, they can sin all they want because Jesus forgives them, and they are promised a good next life. The Christian concept of heaven did not seem as good as *nirvana* to me, though. *Nirvana*, the ultimate goal of every Buddhist, is the total extinction of suffering and the endless cycle of rebirth. It is complete liberation. I have since come to better understand what heaven really is, but back then I thought the Christian heaven was still inside the cycle of suffering and rebirth.

I guess it is not totally true to say that the people in my village did not know *anything* about Jesus. Maybe I should say we did not know anything *true* about Jesus. I have since learned that the local hearsay about Jesus and Christians did contain partial truths, but the small bits of truth were so mixed with lies and distortions that our perception of Jesus was totally disfigured. This is one of the things keeping my people in the dark. Thankfully, one fortunate day, God and a persistent pastor turned the lights on for me.

PASTOR KYAW

The first time I heard about Jesus from someone who actually knew him was after moving to the big city for work. I was barely a teenager, but there were more jobs in the big city than in the village—and they paid more—so I went. Before long, I met Kyaw, a gregarious pastor who could not stop talking about Jesus. Kyaw spoke about Jesus differently than the village gossips had. Kyaw spoke of Jesus as a friend that he wanted to introduce everyone to.

After telling people the good news of Jesus, Pastor Kyaw invited them to learn more at a series of classes. He taught something new about Jesus and salvation each session and invited willing pupils to follow Jesus at the end. Those who believed were baptized and incorporated into his church for ongoing teaching and care. The others were welcome at church too, or free to go. I did not know it at the time, but Pastor Kyaw's strategy was different from other pastors in the area. Many pastors and Christians I have encountered since then focus all their evangelistic energy on pushing for conversion and have little follow-up once the listener repeats a prayer. This leaves new converts to figure out their new life in Christ alone. Whether or not the so-called convert's faith is sincere, this can leave them confused. If Pastor Kyaw had operated that way, my story would be much different—you probably would not be hearing it.

I first observed Pastor Kyaw's conversations about Jesus two or three times from a distance. Then, one day, he approached me and asked my name. I had secretly hoped for this conversation, but now that it was happening, I was not so sure anymore. All the rumors I had heard growing up returned. Why was I talking to this man? Had I forgotten who I was? But it was too late. The exchange had begun; there was no turning back now. Suddenly, without thinking, I blurted out, "I am a Burmese Buddhist," as if he did not know. Pastor Kyaw smiled and kept the conversation moving. After a few encounters, curiosity turned to interest, and I attended one of his classes.

I began Pastor Kyaw's class as an interested skeptic. But each week, as I felt more comfortable with the teacher, I became less defensive. Before long, I felt myself wanting to believe in Jesus. I knew it was impossible for me to believe in Jesus—I was a Burmese Buddhist!—still, I could not deny the feeling. As time passed, I thought I *might* be able to believe in Jesus *one day*—not yet, of course. Then, the impossible day came when I realized I *did* believe in Jesus—the *real* Jesus! And Pastor Kyaw was right. Jesus was nothing like the village rumors!

That is how I got started with Jesus, kind of like the proverbial frog that was slowly boiled before he knew it. Maybe that is a bad analogy—I do not think anyone planned to eat me—I am just saying it was a gradual process that slowly developed until one day I woke up knowing I had changed. After my conversion, Pastor Kyaw unofficially adopted me. I moved in with his family and they treated me like a son. Not only had I gone from being a Buddhist village boy to a Christian city boy, but I even became the son of a pastor! This was an interesting change, but overall, a good one. I learned a lot from my adopted family and the sincere Christians in their circle. A few disorienting hypocrites were mixed in too, but thankfully, I did not get much exposure to them early on. Overall, my new environment proved to be fertile soil for a baby Christian. I was growing by leaps and bounds.

A NEW JOB

A few years into being a Christian, I got a job at a furniture factory. It paid well and required living in the company compound. The housing provision was a perk for many employees, but I already had a good place to live with my adopted dad and was reluctant to move. Still, if I took the job, I would have to move. The new job paid enough to provide for myself and help the family, two things I had always wanted. It seemed like a positive step toward growing up, so I left my first Christian home with a pillow, a small bag of personal items, and a nervous feeling in my stomach.

Nothing in the barebones dormitory made my stomach feel any better. The hot metal building was disheveled and full of hard surfaces—no beds, no mattresses, no chairs—just concrete, steel, and sizzling sheet metal. It felt more like a place for baking bread than for housing humans. Seventeen mats were rolled up on the floor, each shoved against a haphazard cluster of belongings near the wall. "Here is your spot," the manager pointed to a small crack in the clutter, handing me a sleeping mat and blanket roll. Nothing in the dormitory reminded me of *A-may's* house in Anya or Pastor Kyaw's house in the city. The only things that made it feel homey were the few personal items I brought along—a pillow, a bar of soap, a towel, a few sets of clothing, and most importantly, the Bible from Pastor Kyaw and a photo of *A-may*. The move was not easy, but I did not want to stay a kid forever. It was time to grow up. I had made my decision and resolved to stick it out. Still, I could not help asking: "Would this job be worth it? Was I doing the right thing? When would I get to visit home?" I slowly placed my small stack of belongings on the concrete floor between the hot tin wall and my new bedroll. My stoic face hid a flood of second thoughts as I followed the manager into the work zone.

A few months later, I had learned my job, and the big tin oven felt more like home. I worked extra hard to prove myself as good as the older employees and made a practice of always telling the truth. These traits caught the boss's attention, and he steadily gave me more responsibility than the older, more experienced employees. I progressed from one job to another, excelling each time. Finally, the boss put me in charge of signing for materials coming in and inventory going out. Nothing moved in or out of the warehouse without my signature. This put me in a position of authority over people much older than me—something that totally goes against our culture. But I was capable and got used to it—even if it did get to my head a little.

CIRCLES AND VICES

Living at the dorm left little choice for after-hours companions. None of my co-workers were Christian, or if they were, they did not show it. Regardless, there was nobody but each other to shoot air bullets with after dinner. The favorite evening pastimes were cane ball, gambling, and drinking. Whiskey, beer, or at least betel nut were essential to all these activities.

You probably have whiskey and beer in your country, but in case you do not have betel nut, let me introduce one of Myanmar's favorite addictions. Betel nut is the Myanmar equivalent of chewing tobacco—the classic machismo cheek lump that gives a buzz. Picture a hard-faced American cowboy high in the saddle, hat low, pistols hanging. That's how Myanmar people look when they chew betel, except without the saddle, hat, and guns. On the inside we're identical to the cowboy on the movie screen. Betel grows on the Areca palm tree. Its bright red outer shell makes it look like delicious fruit on the tree, but carelessly chomping into it may crack a tooth. On the inside betel is so hard that you need a sharp knife to cut it.

Betel nut preparation begins by coating a betel leaf with white lime paste and placing a few small pieces of its pink and white speckled flesh on top. Each vendor adds a custom combination of tobacco and other ingredients to arrive at their own unique flavor. The leaf is wrapped around the ingredients, producing a thumb-sized quid that perfectly fits in your cheek. Grinding the hard nut package between your molars mixes it with saliva and gives you a buzz. Chew and spit the juice out wherever and whenever you want to, until you are done. Stained teeth, slurred speech, and red juice stains on the ground prove that Myanmar's long-standing betel nut addiction is still going strong. Watch out the first time you try it though! You may be dizzy before you know it.

Back to evenings at the factory. After work it was time to pick your circle and pick your vice—beer, whiskey, or betel. If you wanted to join any of the circles, the accompanying vice was compulsory. I did not want to partake in these vices, but I wanted to join a circle. After internally debating for a few days, I gave in. Neither Jesus nor my adopted father—much less my conscience—approved, but what else was I supposed to do? Sit alone as an outcast every evening? No, that was not an option. I did not feel great about my new habits, but I had no other choice. At least I was not addicted.

I managed well enough until my adopted dad caught wind of things. Pastor Kyaw was worried, and my explanation—"I have no choice, I am not addicted, etc."—did not help. He had invested a lot in me. He loved me like his own son, and he feared that I may never return if I traveled this path much further. Pastor Kyaw immediately started praying and trying to find me a new job. That landed me in a surprising place—the mission field, where a string of unfortunate events turned good news into bad news and a love interest into a murder plot.

GOD SHOT

The peace with God we receive through Christ's gospel also breaks down barriers and makes peace possible between humans—even across hostile and otherwise irreconcilable ethnic, religious, and social lines.

> *In Christ there is not Greek and Jew, circumcision and uncircumcision, barbarian, Scythian, slave and free; but Christ is all and in all. Therefore, as God's chosen ones, holy and dearly loved, put on compassion, kindness, humility, gentleness, and patience, bearing with one another and forgiving one another if anyone has a grievance against another. Just as the Lord has forgiven you, so you are also to forgive. Above all, put on love, which is the perfect bond of unity. And let the peace of Christ, to which you were also called in one body, rule your hearts. And be thankful.*
> (Col 3:11–15)

PERSONAL REFLECTIONS

This is space to write personal discoveries, prayers, or anything else you find helpful. See this chapter's insights for mission in the back of the book or at jesusinthebuddhabelt.com.

10
Murder Plot

Becoming a missionary was not something I had planned for my life, but I was not opposed to it either. When my adopted dad first brought the subject up, I was immediately interested. After all, I am glad someone came to share the gospel with me! Otherwise, I would never have known the blessings of Jesus—forgiveness, peace, hope, a spiritual family, a God who hears my prayers and helps in my difficulties. No one in Anya had these blessings, at least that I knew of. The more I thought and prayed, the more I wanted to become a missionary. My factory job paid better than a missionary salary, but those circles of vice were not good for anyone. It was time for a change. I turned in my resignation letter, said goodbye to a confused boss, and started training as a missionary.

Missionary training covered the basics: how to share the gospel, how to start a church with new believers, and how to avoid getting punched in the face while doing it. The not getting punched part was more intuitive to me than it was to the ethnic minority students from Christian backgrounds. I came from a Burmese Buddhist village. I know how Buddhist people think. I know their values, their hot buttons, and how to deliver a message they can hear. Sometimes my Buddhist background has felt like a hindrance, but it has given me an advantage in communicating the gospel to Buddhists. My Buddhist background has also made me hyper-aware of how much people need Jesus—because I still remember life without him. I could hardly wait for training to end so we could get out there and start sharing the gospel.

At the end of missionary training, a partner and I took our freshly laminated certificates and moved to a little Burmese village not so different from the one I grew up in. We rented a small house with woven bamboo walls, a dirt floor, and a rusty tin roof that leaked a little. It was simple, but sufficient. Sometimes in quiet moments, the little house brought back warm feelings of nostalgia—the sound of *A-may* calling my name, or the fragrance of my favorite curry wafting through the bamboo slits from the outdoor kitchen. Our mission post might have been new, but it was not unfamiliar, at least for me.

My missionary partner and I began our new assignment by praying and getting to know the neighbors. We helped with their work, checked their kids' homework, and did whatever else we could to make friends. Soon we were able to pray for them and introduce Jesus. Many of our village neighbors were not interested, but a few were. Thankfully, no one got angry enough to punch us. After a few months at our new post, a few of the neighbors' demeanor softened and they started asking questions. The progression reminded me of my own journey to Jesus a few years earlier. They learned, experimented with prayer, and counted the cost. Then, before we knew it, we were nurturing a handful of new Burmese believers!

RUNAWAY LOVE

This was an encouraging and abnormal start. Many missionaries labor among the Burmese for years without a single convert, so we were thrilled to see fruit in just a few months. The new believers launched us into a new phase of the mission. We spent less time sharing the gospel with not-yet believers and more time teaching our new brothers and sisters. Things progressed slowly, but surely. Challenges kept coming, but the work was joyful and fulfilling—for me at least. My teammate struggled off and on. He was lonely and not used to spending so much time with Burmese people. Buddhist opposition to the gospel was hard for him too. Still, I thought he was okay. Then, one day, I came home to find him packing his bag. He returned home the next day, and just like that, I was stranded on the mission field.

My home church knew it was not good for me to be alone, so they sent a new mission partner, actually two, but they were not like the one I had before. Surprisingly, this time, the church sent two young ladies. No men were available, so they sent who they had. Thazin and Thin Thin moved into the house I had been living in, and I moved in with a family of new believers. Partnering with two single girls had its challenges, but we kept working the best we could, sometimes together, sometimes apart. Then, before we had finished sorting out our team issues, a bigger problem arose— one of the village girls fell in love with me.

Chit Su was a few years younger than me. She was average height and build. Her dark skin and hair looked just like the other girls in the village. There was really nothing outstanding about her, except that she was drawn to me like a magnet. I was secretly flattered and even slightly attracted to her. Under different circumstances maybe there could have been something between us, but we had a major problem—she was not a Christian. I did not plan to marry yet, but I knew that if I did someday, my wife would have to share my faith. So I pushed Chit Su's love interest out of my mind and tried to focus on my work. Unfortunately, she did not push me out of her mind.

As Chit Su's interest in me grew, she came around more. I tried to be polite but also keep a safe distance. After all, even though we could not pursue a romantic relationship, I had come here to share the gospel, and she needed it too. The village busybodies had a different take on the situation: *528*, the Burmese code number for romantic love. That's the only way their simple minds could see it, and they were not the type who kept their opinions to themselves. Gossip made the problem worse.

The village rumors about Chit Su and me simmered for a few months. Then, one day, the pot boiled. It may be hard for progressive-minded people to understand how black-and-white rural Burmese communities are. With little outside influence, Chit Su's village had been making its own truth for generations. Elders passed down customs as incontrovertible laws without question or competition. The villagers mindlessly accepted them like gravity and air. One law in Chit Su's village states the procedures for beginning marriage by eloping. In this situation, one of the lovers extends a marriage proposal by fleeing the village alone. The other lover may reject the proposal by remaining in the village (to the departed lover's shame) or accept it by following them. If they follow, the village assumes the couple has chosen marriage by sleeping together. There is no discussion and no looking back. The couple must continue with a wedding and all the cultural formalities. This village law got me engaged—unintentionally—and almost got me killed.

One day Chit Su fled the village alone. Anya is not a safe place for young girls to travel alone, so I brought her back. I did this out of concern for her safety. Chit Su and I did *not* sleep together, nor did I plan to marry her. But the village law said otherwise, and it could not be changed. According to the villagers, I had taken their daughter's virginity. That meant we had to marry. And that was that. In their minds, the choice had already been made.

The only escape I could think of was leaving the village. But that would mean a permanent, disgraceful exit from my mission field and a permanent cloak of shame for Chit Su—she would never recover. No one would want to marry her, and the village would forever view me as the irresponsible boy who violated her. What a disaster! I cannot say I did everything perfectly in this situation, but I did *not* sleep with Chit Su, and I simply could *not* marry her. The only thing I could do in good conscience was leave the village in shame, and that is what I resigned to do.

In the meantime, I stayed in the village while the elders and busybodies tried to work things out. On one of those days, Chit Su's brothers planned to settle things the village way—with machetes. Fortunately, they did not find me at home. *Un*fortunately, my hot blood got the best of me, and I picked up my machete to return the favor. Thank God none of that materialized. It did expedite my disgraceful departure from the village though.

I still feel sad when I think about it. I did not want to leave the little flock of new believers yet. I did not want to leave the others I had shared the gospel with. I did not want to leave Chit Su with a ruined reputation either, but I had no choice. I packed my bag, hopped on a friend's motorcycle, and rode back to my home churchwith my tail between my legs.

I do not know what kind of response I expected from the church. I guess I thought they would be angry, maybe kick me out. But while the church leaders were not happy about the village debacle, they were not condemning either. They must have thought I belonged on the mission field because they sent me to another one. The new mission field was a much better situation than the one I left behind, except for the shady mission work happening around me.

CHRISTIAN MINISTRY CORRUPTION

You are probably wondering what kind of shady business could be happening in Christian missions. Well, I wish this part of the story did not exist, but it does. I have seen it with my own eyes. But I need you to know that I am not telling this side of the story flippantly. I tell it with a heavy heart, so that we might avoid more Christ-shaming messes in the future. Shining light in this dark area will help navigate the dangers, toils, and snares of Myanmar mission more effectively—especially for those who are not from our country, since they have a wider linguistic, cultural, and relational gap to cross.

Many of the problems are related to money. A lot of good-hearted foreigners are eager to do mission work in our country, but they do not live here, they do not know the language, and they do not know our people's ways. This requires the foreigners to rely on Myanmar brothers and sisters to bridge the gap. The foreigners bring some helpful things to these partnerships: a desire to spread the gospel, free training events, financial assistance, and other forms of humanitarian relief. Which of these do you think our hand-to-mouth people are most interested in? Unfortunately, the answer is too often money. And coming in at a close second is humanitarian relief. We are also interested in training from foreigners, but it is hard to attend the training without at least a small hope of material gain. I clearly see why the Apostle Paul said, "the love of money is the root of all sorts of evil." Here are some evils that grow from this root in Myanmar.

There are orphanages without orphans. This happens in two ways. Sometimes, so-called orphanages care for children who are not really orphans. This is not bad as long as the donors know the situation. There are many poor children who need care, and it is much better for them to stay with Christians who nurture them in the love of Christ than to grow up in a Buddhist monastery. This situation only poses a problem if the donors are led to believe something untrue in order to widen the crack in their pocketbooks. As long as the donors know the children are not really orphans, all is well. But at times the truth is not made clear.

The other, more problematic way that orphanages without orphans make money is by bringing children to the orphanage only when the donors visit. This happened next door to one of my aunties. I am not sure if this particular "orphanage" explicitly claimed to be Christian, but we assume that most Western donors in our country are. Either way, the orphanage next to my Auntie's house sat empty most of the time. Then, on random days, a crowd of children would show up. The foreigners soon followed with big bags of goodwill. In those days the largest Myanmar currency note was 1,000 Kyat (less than one US dollar at the time). It took multiple bulging bags of cash to make a large donation. Once the orphanage leaders received the money, the donors returned home ... and so did the children, leaving new cars and houses in their wake.

Fraud and embezzlement do not only happen in the orphan business though; winsome personalities leech funds from all kinds of ministry projects—translation, evangelism, church-planting, Bible schools, etc. If the donors do not live here, do not know the language, and do not have good accountability systems, they may never even know their funds have been misused. Reports go back, praises go up, and more funds come over. This lucrative game of Missions Monopoly rewards savvy players with more than play money and plastic houses. God's kingdom is big business with real financial assets to be won. I can hardly tell you without my blood boiling. Somebody needs to crack a whip and flip some tables.

Inflating statistics is also common. I have personally witnessed multiple overlapping ministries all taking credit for the same group of "converts." The ministry groups would participate in an evangelistic outreach together, and each take credit for the results. When twenty people said they believed, each organization reported all twenty, sometimes to the same donor group, so that the total number of new believers reported might be sixty, eighty, or one hundred. This kind of reporting exaggerates numbers and gives credit to people who, many times, have very little—if anything—to do with the fruit. One pastor joked that the whole country has been saved three times over, yet we still have thousands of pagodas, thousands of monks, and thousands of villages without a Christian.

Follow up is another issue. Who took responsibility for teaching the twenty new converts reported above? Sometimes one of the partnering ministries would try to follow up with them. Sometimes no one did. Maybe the donors were not as interested in follow-up as they were in conversion. Maybe the local mission groups did not know that the Great Commission is to make disciples—not just converts. Or maybe ongoing follow-up and discipleship is just harder and less glorious than evangelistic events. I do not know all the reasons these things happen . . . I am just sad that they do.

I also saw immorality among pastors and missionaries. Do not get me wrong—we are all capable of sin, myself included. The sin itself is not the problem; the problem is how we handle it. Some ministers are famous for it. I once met a missionary from one of the ethnic minorities whose pattern was to enter a new field, preach the gospel, win a few converts, and commit adultery with one of the local women. This happened multiple times. Instead of facing church discipline, this man was moved to a new mission field each time like nothing ever happened, allowing the cycle to repeat. How terrifying it must be to answer to God for this! I left the furniture factory to escape circles of vice, but in the world of Christian mission, even more grotesque vices masqueraded in Jesus's name.

SECOND EXODUS

On top of these depressing discoveries, I started having disagreements with another minister. If I told you the issue, you would laugh ... or cry. You know how it is when you get sideways with a person and cannot get straight. This brother and I could not see eye to eye and could not agree to disagree. Talking made things worse, so we went silent. That did not help either. Eventually, things got so heated that I had to get out—not permanently—just long enough to cool down and regain perspective in the big city. Two cans of Dagon beer and one cigarette seemed like an easy way to release some pent-up frustration. But they ended up being an easy release from my second mission field instead. I know, as a minister, I should not have done this, but I was angry and did not care. And I did *not* get drunk.

My superiors had already been getting misconstrued—if not dishonest—reports about me from the minister I was at odds with. This incident pushed them over the edge. Unlike many shady people doing Christian mission work, my pastor was an honest, God-fearing man. He believed in taking action to root problems out, not covering them up by moving the culprits to different mission fields. So Pastor Kyaw shipped me halfway across the country to a rehab center.

Shame and sadness escorted me to the overnight bus that afternoon. I plopped into my seat without even speaking to the person next to me. I did not look at him. I did not look out the window in his direction. I did not look out the other window. The only place I looked was down ... at the floor. And I did it with my head hung mighty low. My first mission field had ended in disaster, but I was given another chance. Now my second mission field had evaporated along with my hopes for redemption. Whether or not I would ever get a third chance, I did not know. These thoughts swam in my weary mind for hours as I stared at the floor. Meanwhile, the bus was transporting me to a new world. I did not know anything about where I was going, but I did not care. I was too busy lamenting the past to wonder about the future. Even if I had been thinking about the future, though, I could never have guessed how much lower my head would hang and how much longer I would want to stare at the floor.

GOD SHOT

God appears absent in this chapter, but by faith we know that he sees—and is grieved by—every sinful action. God is presently exercising unfathomable patience, but he *will* certainly deliver justice at the proper time.

> *Be silent before the Lord and wait expectantly for him; do not be agitated by one who prospers in his way, by the person who carries out evil plans. Refrain from anger and give up your rage; do not be agitated—it can only bring harm. For evildoers will be destroyed, but those who put their hope in the Lord will inherit the land.*
>
> (Ps 37:7–9)

PERSONAL REFLECTIONS

This is space to write personal discoveries, prayers, or anything else you find helpful. See this chapter's insights for mission in the back of the book or at jesusinthebuddhabelt.com.

11
Inside Addiction

After a long night winding through the mountains, it was time to stop staring at the floor and raise my head. I climbed down from the bus into a new world. The hot, arid plains of Burmese-populated Anya were long gone. My feet now stood on a frigid, fertile mountain of ethnic diversity. Sleep-deprived and starving, the first thing on my mind was breakfast, the second was a jacket. But before I found either of those, Z, my escort to the rehab center, found me. Breakfast and warm clothes would have to wait. I swung a leg over the back of Z's motorcycle, duffle bag in hand. "Hold on!" he yelled, and we were off. The trip was only half an hour, but time crawls when you are hungry and cold. All I could do was hold onto Z as we wound further and further into the mountains on smaller and smaller roads. Finally, the dirt path ended at the rehab center.

I came to rehab to overcome my addiction. The only problem was, I did not have an addiction. But that did not matter. When your superiors say a thing is true, it is. Rehab was the reward for my self-confessed two beers and a cigarette. I had to accept it. At least it was a chance to study the Bible more. I would try to stay focused on that.

"Sit here," Z said as he dropped me off, pointed to a chair, and then disappeared. I followed my only instruction and waited in the cold. A distant cock-a-doodle announced the first rays of morning light spilling over the horizon as I waited. Other than my empty stomach and shivering bones, waiting wasn't bad. My peaceful moment ended as one of the teachers walked around the corner. "Follow me," he said, and we were off on a campus tour. The teacher pointed as we walked: a crude kitchen and dining area, a garden, a meeting hall, a volleyball court, and, finally, a bunkhouse. I flashed back to the hot tin building at the furniture factory. The two buildings had one thing in common—bedding for a bunch of people. Everything else was different. For starters, the bunkhouse was cool. This was partly because of the weather, and partly because it was wrapped with thatch and bamboo instead of corrugated tin. The bunkhouse had beds—ten wooden bunks stacked on top of each other. And, best of all, the bunkhouse had windows, two of them, both with scenic mountain views. I spotted an empty upper bunk one bed away from the door with a folded blanket. "That one is yours," my tour guide said. "Put your bag down and come eat some breakfast."

The smell of steamed rice and hot eggs hit my nostrils before I rounded the corner into the dining area. Most of the addicts were already eating at a long, wooden table when we walked in. The teacher handed me a hot plate and ushered me to the head of the table. "Everybody, welcome Lin. He got here this morning." Smiling, smug, caring, indifferent: all kinds of faces returned my conflicted gaze. "*Mingalaba*," I greeted them, with a forced smile. So began my rehab adventure with nineteen total strangers, a plate of steamed rice, and a hard-fried egg.

A month later, Teacher Brang caught me in a solitary moment, "Lin, you do not look like you belong here. What is your story?" I was glad he could tell me apart from the addicts. He seemed genuine, so I opened up. Teacher Brang believed my story and told me his. Like many Kachin men, he struggled with addiction until Jesus saved him from opium and helped get his life together. Teacher Brang had even visited Anya on mission trips and knew where my village was. The two of us built a bond over the following months. In fact, Teacher Brang later got me out of rehab before the required year was over, but we are not to that part of the story yet.

In the meantime, I studied and worked hard. The rehab center had been carved out of the jungle just a few years earlier, so there was plenty of physical labor to do. We constructed a new building, grew some of our food, and had group Bible lessons and private study time each day. Throwing myself into these activities helped the time pass and kept me from feeling sorry for myself. Then, one day, Teacher Brang pulled me aside and said, "Lin, would you like to join the missionary training school?" I quickly thought through the implications. I had already been to a missionary training school. I would rather go back to the mission field, but who would send an "addict" fresh out of rehab? I decided that mission school was my best option. Maybe after graduation, I could return to the mission field. At least mission school would get me out of jungle isolation. I agreed and moved to the school a few days later, along with several others who were finishing rehab.

A NEW START WITH BO

Mission school got me out of rehab early. It also gave me a new partner and another chance at redemption. Sure, my first two mission assignments left a few bumps and bruises, but they also taught me a lot. Things would be different this time—*good* different. By God's grace, my third mission field would not tragically tailspin like the others. I had failed twice, but this time I was ready to pass the test. I did not want to stay a kid forever!

My partner, Bo, was a recent convert from Buddhism. He grew up in a rich family and entered a Buddhist monastery as a young man. All was well for him—until drugs. Drugs got their hooks into Bo and would not let go. The monk robe was no deterrent. Bo and drugs abused each other until the senior monks gave up and expelled him from the monastery. Things got much worse after that before they got better. By the end, Bo had lost everything but his life—and he nearly lost that a few times too. Finally, one day, a God-sent stranger lifted Bo's strung-out face off the ground and uttered three shocking words that Sunday School kids take for granted, "Jesus loves you."

"Is there really someone in this world who still loves me?" Bo asked in disbelief. "Of course there is," the stranger continued. "No matter what you do, Jesus will never stop loving you." Suddenly, years of pent-up anger and frustration broke Bo's stoic tear ducts, leaving a thin trail of clean skin down the middle of both soiled cheeks. But more than Bo's cheeks were cleansed that day. Those tears were like the sun reappearing after a long, dark night. Light had finally come. A new day—no, a new life—was beginning. Bo met Jesus right there, beside the road, and began the long process of recovery.

Bo was already in the rehab program when I showed up cold and hungry. Like me, he was the only person there from his tribe. Most of the other men were Kachin, and all Kachin grew up as Christians, at least in name. Bo and I were Christians now, but we grew up Buddhist. The Kachin also had their own language. They spoke to Bo and me in Burmese, but the rest of the conversations were in their own language. Bo had been around the Kachin longer and understood some of what they said, but for me, it was total gibberish. At times I could tell they were talking about me. Some of the Kachin brothers treated us kindly, but we still felt like oddballs, not sharing their language, culture, or Christian heritage. This kept Bo and me on the outside looking in. But we were outside together, and that is how we became friends.

The rehab center taught me some hard lessons about being an ethnic minority. This was difficult for a Burmese, especially one from Anya—I had always been in the proud majority and liked it that way. Being Burmese felt like an advantage, until rehab. There, it felt like a disadvantage in every way. My language, my culture, my skin color, and my religious background were all unwanted and considered inferior. Becoming a marginalized minority was harder than I expected, but it gave me more compassion for the ethnic groups I had once looked down on.

Back to our new mission field. This was Bo's first go-round, and he was still a pretty new believer. I expected some growing pains but thought he would handle them maturely, since he was more than a decade older than me. I was right about the pains and wrong about the maturity. Several Kachin brothers at the mission school had warned me about Bo: "Are you sure you want to partner with Bo? You know how he is." I knew part of their warning was skewed by racial bias; the other part, though, was based on his erratic behavior. I ignored the first part and strongly considered the second. But who was I to throw stones at Bo? We all have our issues. I wanted to be a missionary and I needed a partner to do it. Bo was the only one I had, so perfect or not, we moved to a nearby mountain town to share the gospel and start a church.

ADJUSTMENTS

My new mission field was nothing like Anya. Thankfully, the rehab center and mission school had prepared me for it. My Burmese face was in the minority here. The temperatures were cooler, with more rain and less dust than Anya. The land was more fertile here too, which meant better crops and better incomes. And, of course, the culture was different. The only thing similar to Anya was the rental house. Its woven bamboo walls, rusty metal roof, and outside kitchen felt like old friends. Everything in the rental house was familiar, except the cement floor. That was a nice upgrade from the house I grew up in. More important than the house though, was what it allowed us to do. It was a base for sharing the hope of Jesus in our new mission field.

I was already seeing telltale signs of the future during the first few months in our new home. Living alone with Bo was ... interesting. Sometimes he treated me like a friend. Other times he treated me like a personal servant for cooking, cleaning, bringing an item across the room, or whatever he did not want to do. Sometimes Bo treated me with respect. Other times he treated me like a stupid kid. Sometimes he was patient and kind. Other times he flew off the handle, yelling and threatening violence.

I tried to give Bo as much grace and understanding as I could. We were from different backgrounds. He grew up in the mountains of luxury; I grew up in the plains of poverty. He was worshipped as a monk; I was overlooked as a layperson. His people used little oil with their curry; mine used little curry with our oil. His culture thought my people were rude; my culture thought his people were hillbillies. I could go on, but you get the point. Lots of things made our partnership difficult. But Bo and I had something powerful in common, too—we both knew Jesus. By grace, Jesus had rescued us from sin and changed our lives. This common experience transcended our differences, and I hoped it would be enough to hold our partnership together.

At first, Bo's episodes were sporadic and mild, but they grew more frequent and intense over time. This made living with Bo hard, but I tried to stay positive. Maybe passing this test was a fast track to maturity. At least viewing the situation this way helped me embrace it as a growth opportunity instead of getting discouraged. The importance of the mission helped me stay focused too. Putting up with a few headaches at home was no big deal if it allowed me to share the gospel in a place that needed it. I tried to trust that God put me with Bo for a reason, stay focused on what mattered, and let the rest go. This worked fairly well ... most of the time. A few times, though, I lost my cool and let Bo have it right back.

I believe Bo really had been given a new heart—I saw signs of it, even if rough edges obscured it. He needed someone to help overcome his struggles, not someone to throw stones at him. I tried to be a friend rather than a judge. After all, are we not all at different places in our growth journey? Working with Bo was difficult, but I believed God had a plan for it. I also did not want a third shameful departure from the mission field, which was another reason to make it work.

A PHONE CALL I WILL NEVER FORGET

The next few months Bo spiraled into schizophrenic cycles. He got angry, made peace, then got angry again. This happened multiple times most days. This continued until I took a trip home to sort out a few family matters. Bo stayed in our new town, living in the little bamboo house alone—probably the first time he had been alone since before rehab. I was busy with family and did not give Bo's situation much thought until a few days later when the phone rang with news I will never forget. It was Tan, one of the Christian brothers in our new town. His sober voice skipped the pleasantries and got straight to the point: "Little brother, you have got to come back. Bo is in bad shape." I did not know what had happened, but I knew I had to get back as soon as possible. Bo was in trouble and there was no one else to help.

I abruptly wrapped things up with my family and boarded the first bus back to our mission field that evening. All night, I wondered what had happened, as the bus wound back up the chilly, green mountains. I prayed all the way—wondered and prayed, trying to wonder less and pray more. When the prayers ran out, I searched the Bible for comfort, wisdom, a word from God—anything to calm my mind. Finally, the bus's airbrakes released at my destination.

Resolute and nervous, I immediately called Tan. He showed up a few minutes later on a motorcycle ... with fewer words than usual. No, "Good morning," no, "How are you?" All Tan said was, "Let us go to my house, Little Brother." The words slowly started coming once we sat in his living room—words that he did not want to say and I did not want to hear. Tan was surprisingly composed as he described how Bo's life had spun out of control over the past few days. But I could feel the raw nerves beneath the surface, especially when he got to Bo's drunken episode at his house. At that point, Tan paused and looked out the window. Then he stared directly into my eyes: "Bo is a totally different person than we knew. I was afraid of what he might do to my wife and children."

Things with Bo were even worse than I expected. It is hard to imagine how wildly out of control his life became in less than a week—unless you understand the devastating power of addiction, that is. Bo's descent into darkness started with an old friend and a bottle of beer. One bottle turned into two, two turned into three, and by then it was too late—Bo was on a downhill slide and could not stop. In the following days, he was back to drugs, back to the bar, back to the whorehouse, and God only knows where else.

It was day three or four of Bo's tailspin before Tan providentially discovered him. Tan just happened to spot Bo in a drinking establishment while running errands nearby. He offered to take Bo home. Bold and uninhibited, Bo slurred back insults about Tan and God that I cannot bear to repeat. There was nothing

Tan could do but go home and pray. Then, later that day, Bo showed up at Tan's house demanding money and threatening to hurt his family if he did not get it. Tan solemnly described how Bo appeared that day: the careless rage in his eyes, the vulgar, drooling speech, and the gestures and threats of violence. That is when he decided to call me for help.

CRASH AND BURN

The next few days spent trying to corral Bo were a living hell. His week-long binge was destroying himself and everything around him. He could not be reasoned with. He could not be contained. And, eventually, he could not even be found. For the next few days, Bo would randomly show up somewhere acting a fool—drunk, high, and cursing—demanding money and shaming the name of Christ. Then, he would disappear until he ran out of booze or cash. Tan and I did not want to get law enforcement involved—it was too shameful. Everybody in town knew we were Christian missionaries, How would this reflect on our cause? At the same time, things were getting worse by the minute, and we had to do something fast. Finally, after depleting every spiritual, physical, and mental resource at our disposal, we shamefully reported Bo to the police, and they joined the search effort. But either the *Law of Cause and Effect* or the hand of Almighty God got to him before the rest of us.

The news hit me like a brick wall: "This morning an unidentified body was found on Pagoda Hill. It sounds like Bo."

Have you ever had the feeling where all your senses get foggy at the same time? You feel pressure against your skin, but your body is numb. You see images, but they are out of focus. You hear sounds, but they are muffled and distant. It is like being underwater. That is how I spent the next slow-motion moments. Memories of Bo swam across my muted consciousness for what felt like an hour of silent oblivion. "He is at the morgue now. You can go check," the city official's voice snapped me back to reality. Off we went to the final stop in our search, a place I never want to visit again.

The dingy, ramshackle building was almost as chilling as the corpse itself. Seeing the dead body was hard, but smelling it was even worse. I will never forget the cocktail stench of body odor, alcohol, and death. We reluctantly inched closer, peering at the strange, breathless figure—feet, legs, torso, arms, face. I stared hard at the face. Could it be? Memories from mission school and the rehab center flashed in front of me . . . Bo sharing his testimony, telling a joke, laughing, eating in the dining hall. I looked again. Yes, it was Bo. But the lifeless body on the table looked nothing like the mission partner I moved here with a few months earlier. This man had lost the dignity of clothing. His full head of thick, black hair was roughly razored off. The color was gone from his face and the pale, bristly flesh that remained was cracked and swollen. God, I wish I could forget that image—but I never will. Suddenly, my gut and my heart could not take any more. I had to turn away.

GOING HOME

Walking away from that corpse ended my third mission field. What a life I have had as a Christian missionary! I left a sufficient paycheck at the furniture factory to serve God and escape circles of vice, yet what did I find in the mission field—not one time, not two times, but three? It was enough to make anyone want to quit God's work—enough to make an unsure person even want to quit being a Christian. Where could I go from here? I could leave the mission field, but I could not leave God. No matter how many sinners may be in the church, I knew God was real. Jesus was my constant Companion and Savior. I had nowhere else to go for refuge. But what was I to do now? I could not stay in this mission field any longer, but I could not go back to the mission profiteering system in the big city either.

After lots of thought, counsel, and conflicted deliberation, I did the only reasonable thing—hit the eject button and went home. I did not go home holding my head high though. No, my head hung mighty low, lower than it had on the bus ride to rehab even, but for different reasons. This time I had done nothing wrong. I was forced to leave this mission field because of someone else's mistakes. And, this time, I was not headed for a new mission field or a rehab center in the mountains. There was only one place left I could go—home.

Normally, I loved to go home, but not this time—not this way. I wanted to go home with something to show for it, something my family and village could be proud of. Instead, I was going home empty-handed, without succeeding at what I set out to do. What a laughable failure! That is not how I wanted to go home, but it is how I *had to*. Thank God that at least my home was a safe place. By that time my mother and sisters had all come into God's family, so I would at least have their sympathy. That would be nice. Sympathy, *nga-pi*, and *A-may's* cooking could work wonders. Home was just the rehab center I needed, the perfect place to recover from my real addiction—missionary trauma.

I did not phone to tell *A-may* I was coming. I could not bear to. I just stuffed my bag, caught a ride to the bus station, and bought a ticket. The winding, bumpy bus was a good place to think. Our physical descent from the mountains mirrored my emotional descent on the inside. Hadn't the Almighty sent me here to accomplish his good purposes? Then why was the devil running up the score? Thank God I did not have to get all my conflicting thoughts sorted on the way home. It would take much longer than a bus ride for that.

Finally, the air brakes released. I silently stepped off the bus into a sea of pushy taxi drivers. The warm Anya breeze soon blew across my face on the back of a motorcycle taxi. Paved roads turned into dirt roads and dirt roads turned into trails. At last, the driver stopped and spit betel nut in front of my childhood home. I climbed off with my head spinning. How would I explain this to *A-may*? But before I could plan the first sentence—much less speak it—*A-may* had made it across the yard and wrapped her arms around me. It was like she already knew. The long story would come later. For the moment it was enough to be home, home in Mother's arms.

GOD SHOT

Though God's role in Bo's death is not certain, we know that at times God has disciplined his people by taking their lives (Lev 10:1–2; Acts 5:1–11; 1 Cor 11:29–32).

> Anyone who disregarded the law of Moses died without mercy, based on the testimony of two or three witnesses. How much worse punishment do you think one will deserve who has trampled on the Son of God, who has regarded as profane the blood of the covenant by which he was sanctified, and who has insulted the Spirit of grace? For we know the one who has said, "Vengeance belongs to me; I will repay," and again, "The Lord will judge his people." It is a terrifying thing to fall into the hands of the living God.
>
> (Heb 10:28–31)

PERSONAL REFLECTIONS

This is space to write personal discoveries, prayers, or anything else you find helpful. See this chapter's insights for mission in the back of the book or at jesusinthebuddhabelt.com.

12
Going Deeper:
A Prince, the Bride, and Jesus

Where I grew up in Anya, we did not know anything *true* about Jesus. Everybody in my village knew rumors and half-truths, along with some outright lies. But what else were we to believe? No one told us the truth. I now know that faith comes by hearing—hearing the word of Christ. But my people did not hear the word of Christ. Nobody came to tell us. All we heard about Jesus was distortions and rumors. I believe the main reason more Buddhists are not turning to Jesus is that they have not heard the true message of Christ. There are other problems as well, but those do not come into play until after the gospel is communicated.

This may be hard to believe, but many Anya villages have never had a Christian witness at all. Let me say this another way—many Burmese Buddhists live and die without ever hearing the gospel even once. That is the first problem. How can they believe a gospel they have not heard? The Apostle Paul says they cannot (Rom 10:13–17). Not hearing the gospel is the first reason many of our Buddhist brothers and sisters cannot believe and be saved. They are still waiting for a pair of beautiful feet. But there are other problems keeping our Buddhist brothers and sisters in the dark as well.

Some villages have heard the gospel from Christians who contradict the message with their lives. In this case, the Christians had good talk, but a bad walk. We have sayings about things like this in Burmese:

> *Your mouth cries "God," but your hand cries "flesh."*
>
> *Easy to say; hard to do.*

The problem of Christian hypocrisy is much more difficult to remedy than the problem of people who have never heard the gospel. If people have not heard the message, all we must do is go tell them. But if someone has preached Jesus with their mouth and denied him with their life, the gospel has become an immunization rather than a healing medicine. The audience who has heard a dishonest witness to the gospel is even harder to persuade than those who have never heard in the first place.

Hypocrisy gives Buddhists great evidence for discrediting Jesus. Maybe that is why the devil seems particularly keen on this strategy, directly aiming his schemes against the moral character of those who preach the gospel. And he too often succeeds, keeping the hearers in the dark, separated from Christ. Our Buddhist brothers and sisters will only know the love of Christ if Christians tell them with our lips *and* show them with our lives.

A third problem that I see keeping many Burmese Buddhists from Jesus is the way the message is preached. Sometimes a village receives the true message of Christ's gospel from a person whose life also commends it. Praise God for this! I wish every village in Anya could have this blessing! But sometimes, even with both of these elements in place, the messenger fails to communicate the gospel clearly. In this case, the problem may be that the Christian does not know the truth of Buddhism well enough to communicate the truth of Christ in a way that is meaningful to the audience. I realize this might sound like a blasphemous statement to many Christians, but let me explain.

BUDDHIST TRUTH BRIDGES

Please do not think I am saying that Jesus and Buddha are equally true. They are not. Christ is *the* Truth—Buddha is *not*. Christ's teaching is *all* true—Buddha's is *not*. Christ *alone* can save from sin and death—Buddha *cannot*. I am not saying that Jesus and Buddha are equal in status or that they are equally true. What I *am* saying is that *parts* of Buddhism are true. Some things the Buddha said are true. Some of his teachings are similar to the Bible. However, some of the Buddha's teachings are also drastically different from the Bible—in these cases, we must go with the Bible. I am not asking anyone to go against the perfect truth of God's Word—please *do not do that!*

All of Buddhism is *not* true, but Buddhism does *contain* truth. I bring this up for one reason only: I think that many Christians could explain Christ to Buddhists more clearly if they better understood the Buddha's teaching. Why? Because parts of Buddha's teaching powerfully point to Jesus. "Why do we need to use the Buddha's teaching to point people to Jesus?" you may ask. Because people are more likely to explore something they do not yet believe if it is supported by something they believe already. People may not base their decision about Jesus totally on logic, but they need to know that Jesus is a logical possibility. Here are a few examples of Buddhist teachings that can point people to Jesus.

Four of Buddhism's Five Precepts are directly from the Ten Commandments: 1) don't kill, 2) don't steal, 3) don't commit adultery, 4) don't lie. In the beginning, the Five Precepts can help Buddhists understand their sin and need for a savior. Later on, the Five Precepts can also point them back to the rest of the Ten Commandments which relate to God and parents.

The *Law of Karma*, properly understood, keeps Buddhists trapped in an inescapable cycle of suffering due to their bad actions (*ka-ya' kan*), words (*wuzi' kan*), and thoughts (*ma-naw kan*). They cannot resolve this on their own. But what if someone with no bad *karma* came to rescue them?

Buddhism teaches a fiery hell. Even though hell is not eternal in Buddhism, many Buddhists are afraid of it because of their sin. Jesus guarantees eternal heaven instead of eternal hell for all who believe in him.

Do you see how the process works? Take a truth that the people already accept, and point them to Jesus whom they do not yet accept. This will not coerce anyone into the kingdom, but it can build a helpful common ground to start the conversation. True, lots of things in Buddhism do not line up with Jesus's teaching.

I am not suggesting we accept those things. I am suggesting that, in many cases, we can more clearly communicate the gospel of Jesus to our Buddhist brothers and sisters if we understand their teaching and use it as a bridge to Jesus instead of ignoring or just arguing against it.

This is a sensitive area that some Christians are uncomfortable with. And that is okay. Some Christians, whom I highly respect, sternly warn against making any reference to Buddhism when sharing the gospel. Sometimes, these brothers and sisters are still able to effectively communicate the message of Jesus. In that case, I have no argument with them. But even though these ministers do not explicitly reference Buddhist teachings when they share the gospel, I think they understand basic Buddhist concepts—and this helps them communicate clearly. This group is not ignorant of Buddhism—they just choose not to explicitly mention it. That is an important distinction. Some Christians do not know anything about Buddhism. These people usually do not share the gospel, but I have seen a few attempts. In the best case, these people fail to powerfully communicate the message. In the worst case, they unnecessarily offend or confuse the audience.

At this point you may be thinking: "Can God not use even our most imperfect attempts to share the gospel?" Of course he can! Thank God that he can—and he does—otherwise he would not be able to use any of us! Obedience to share the gospel is the main thing. But do we not also want to love our hearers by giving them the best possible chance to understand what we are saying? Do not "both the Spirit *and* the bride say, 'Come!'" (Rev 22:17)? And if we are part of how God bids people to come, do we not want to "proclaim it clearly, as [we] should" (Col 4:4)?

I think we all agree that obedience to share the gospel is key. The Holy Spirit's work is key. Prayer is key. Do not skip these parts! In addition to these things, I am suggesting that we can also use parts of Buddhism to build bridges to Jesus. Of course, if you are going to do this, you should take the time to really understand Buddhism. If not, you will get into trouble. Maybe that is why some Christians are reluctant to tread here. It is also important to steer clear of badmouthing other religions. That is disrespectful. How would we feel if someone started badmouthing Jesus? For me, comparison or denigration is not the point. The point is to use your audience's previously accepted truth as a bridge to Jesus. I do this naturally because I used to be Buddhist. This is also how I understand Paul's message to the Athenians on Mars Hill. He quotes their Greek poets and religion to establish common ground. Then he points from the thing they already know to the thing they do not yet know—Jesus (Acts 17:22–34).

Here's an example. How do you convince a Buddhist of their sin? Some Christians say that Buddhists will not admit their sin. I have never experienced this problem. The Judson Burmese Bible itself uses many different words for sin, but most Christians typically limit their vocabulary to just one word: *a-pyit*. The Christians who say Buddhists will not admit their sin quote a Bible verse with that word in it. I use that word sometimes too, but not *only* that word and not *only* that verse. A variety of words for sin are burned into the Buddhist conscience that are impossible for an honest person to deny. In this case, I use Buddhist teaching to show people that they are sinners. This is a biblical truth that is also found in Buddhism, but it is easier for them to understand and accept this truth through the lens they are looking through.

THE PERSISTENT PRINCE

There are also Buddhist stories that I use to teach biblical truths. Buddhist people are trained to reject the concept of a savior and rely solely on themselves. This is a huge barrier between them and Jesus! Sometimes I use a story from one of the Buddha's previous lives (*Zat-taw*) to show that we all need a savior. In this story, the Buddha-to-be is a rich prince named *Maha Zanaga*. He is often portrayed in paintings at monasteries and is baked into ceramic tile at the *Shwedagon* pagoda. The story is widely known; most people will start nodding their heads as soon as you begin telling it.

The gist of the story is this: The young prince *Zanaga* sets off on a long journey by ship. One tragic day, the ship starts to sink. While everyone else is panicking, *Maha Zanaga* lathers himself with oil and climbs to the highest part of the mast. He courageously leaps into the ocean and starts swimming. Seven days later, long after everyone else has drowned, *Maha Zanaga* is still swimming. What incredible perseverance! Yet despite his perseverance, *Maha Zanaga* still finds himself in the middle of the ocean with nothing but water in every direction. Death seems like the only possible outcome, until the glorious moment when *Mani Mekhala* comes to the rescue. After proudly refusing her help the first time, *Maha Zanaga* accepts her second offer and is saved.

Buddhists use this story to teach the value of perseverance, but it also demonstrates the *need for more* than perseverance. If *Mani Mekhala* had not come to the rescue, *Maha Zanaga* would have drowned in the middle of the ocean. His perseverance was commendable—what a man to swim for six days straight!—but he only lived to tell the tale because *Mani Mekhala* came to save him. If such an amazing swimmer needed a savior, how much more do we, who are drowning in sin, unable to keep the commandments? If a person agrees to this, we have overcome a major objection. This story can help our audience be more open to a meaningful conversation about Jesus as Savior, rather than shrugging us off as ignorant and irrelevant.

The Buddhist story of *Maha Zanaga* builds a bridge to Jesus by showing our need for him. It does not force anyone to walk across that bridge, but it creates an opportunity they may not have seen before. In other words, stories like this do not guarantee our audience will be open to the gospel—that is between them and the Holy Spirit—but it can remove barriers and establish common ground. I believe this is a good start.

THE PERSISTENT BRIDE

I began by sharing three reasons for gospel poverty in Anya. The first is that no one has come to preach the gospel in many of our villages. Christian brothers and sisters, let us please pray and work to end this problem! The second problem is that the messenger sometimes immunizes the audience by contradicting the gospel with their behavior. Lord help us end this problem too! I also suggested a third problem: sometimes well-meaning Christians do not communicate the gospel effectively, because they do not understand their Buddhist audience. True, talking about Buddhism is not necessary—sharing the gospel is! But should we not use every possible means to communicate it more clearly?

I think the *Maha Zanaga* story poses a challenge for Christians as well. The prince was still alive seven days after the ship sank because of his perseverance. His perseverance did not save him, but it did put him in a position to receive salvation. Christian brothers and sisters, maybe our perseverance can put our Buddhist friends in a position to receive salvation—perseverance to pray, perseverance to share the gospel, perseverance to communicate clearly. If God has truly chosen to offer salvation through both the Spirit *and* the bride's invitation, then may we be found a persevering bride, never ceasing to bid them "Come!" And may the Spirit help us to do this with clarity, offering our Buddhist friends every possible chance to understand, believe, and be saved by Jesus.

GOD SHOT

God has sovereignly assigned his people two indispensable links in the chain leading others to salvation:

1. Preaching—announcing the good news of salvation through Jesus
2. Sending—setting apart and helping others go and announce the good news

Without these two links, the chain cannot go further.

> For everyone who calls on the name of the Lord will be saved.
>
> How, then, can they call on him they have not believed in?
> And how can they believe without hearing about him?
> And how can they hear without a preacher?
> And how can they preach unless they are sent?
>
> As it is written: How beautiful are the feet of those who bring good news.
>
> (Rom 10:13–15)

PERSONAL REFLECTIONS

This is space to write personal discoveries, prayers, or anything else you find helpful. See this chapter's insights for mission in the back of the book or at jesusinthebuddhabelt.com.

DISCUSSION AND PRAYER GUIDE

This was the final chapter in Lin's story. See the Discussion and Prayer Guide in the back of this book for deeper personal or group reflection or scan the QR code for an online version.

jesusinthebuddhabelt.com
Also scan this QR code to:

 SHARE your thoughts or ask a question

 EXPLORE the topics of this book further with free articles, photos, videos, and recipes

 CONNECT with ongoing mission initiatives in the Buddha Belt

Part 4

Tha Gyi's Story

UNPRECEDENTED OPPORTUNITY IN THE URBAN YOUTH SCENE

Tha Gyi snaps a proud selfie from his temporary home abroad

13
Yangon City Lights

Dark and light, day and night, betel nut and breath mints—so far my half-lived life has been stacked high with contrasts. I went from a dusty, rural village to a tidy metropolis abroad. From a dirt floor to a handsome salary. From Burmese language to English and Chinese. The contrasts in my life keep stacking up like bricks on a wall—up, up, up till it's hard to see over the top. But I still haven't mentioned the biggest contrast of all: I was first born from a Buddhist woman, then reborn from a Jewish man. Shocked? Me too! The first birth brought me close to family and friends. The second birth took me farther from them. My Great Wall of Contrasts was off to a good start even before meeting Jesus—since then it has outgrown the Great Wall of China.

Brick upon brick, upon brick, the contrasts between my past and present have taken me farther and farther from home. In quiet moments, I still feel the longing in my gut. Sometimes it passes after a few seconds—sometimes it lingers for weeks. But the wicker bamboo walls I grew up in, the smell of *nga-pi* on the dinner table, Dad's warm laughter, and the pungent taste of pickled tea salad are never far from my mind. Still, I'm not sure when I'll make it back home. I guess I'm not sure about a lot of things these days. I am sure of one thing though—my name is still Tha Gyi, "Oldest Son." This name comes with a long list of responsibilities. Providing for the family, setting an example for younger siblings, and taking care of parents in old age all fall on me. Tha Gyi is a heavy load, but it's an honor to carry for the family, even if it has taken me far from home.

YANGON INTERNET CAFES

I laid the first bricks on my Great Wall of Contrasts in Yangon in 2005. It was hard adjusting to the big city as a teenage immigrant from Nowhere, but the decision to move was easy. There's nothing to do in the village. Okay, there's a lot to do—just nothing interesting, nothing that feels like progress. If I stayed in the village, I was doomed to plant rice like my parents and grandparents. That was fine for them, but this is a new era. People who stay in the village get left in the past. The rest of us are chasing the path of upward mobility to the biggest city possible, ideally in a foreign country. People who go abroad make big salaries and can send money to their families at home. Some even save enough to build a house or start a business when they return. That was my dream. And Yangon was my first step.

The Yangon I moved to in 2005 was much different than Yangon today. For starters, the internet was nearly non-existent. I first heard of it as a rumor. Supposedly, foreign visitors could send electronic mail (whatever that was) from a few select hotel lobbies. Later, internet cafes popped up and I got to experience the mysterious World Wide Web firsthand. I still remember how out of place I felt walking into an internet cafe for the first time. A friend and I reluctantly opened the door, peered at the dozen or so computers inside, and nearly bolted for home before trying it. But before we could escape, the host swooped in and ushered us to a seat. This solved one problem and introduced another—neither of us had any idea what to do once we sat in front of the computer. But before we could craft a second escape plan, the host opened Internet Explorer, created our first chat accounts, and showed us how the mouse worked. An hour later, we floated home like astronauts on the moon—well worth the thirty-cent investment to ride the razor-edge of technology.

We hardly knew how to fill that first hour in the internet cafe, but we soon found ourselves squinting in front of the screen for hours on end. Accessing information, games, and conversations from outside Myanmar for the first time was exhilarating!

The ancient technology of telephone cables brought megabytes into the internet cafe at a snail's pace. Sometimes, the connection would drop altogether. You never knew if it was gone for a quick smoke break or an out-of-town vacation. The cafe workers didn't know either. Thankfully, they *did* know how to fix most other problems though. And they were the *only* ones who understood the complex web of servers, proxies, and firewalls back then. I experienced their magic powers the first time my web browser stopped responding. One of the cafe workers came to the rescue, entering strings of memorized numbers and right-clicking "refresh" like a frightened machine gunner. We internet illiterates watched in awe, hoping the incantation would get our chat boxes going again ... and sometimes it did.

We didn't understand the extent of the military's death grip on our web browsing back then because we didn't know any different. No one cared that foreign news sites and YouTube were blocked. We had never seen them. We were blind without knowing it because we'd never seen the sun—and we'd never talked to anyone who had. I still remember watching military atrocities on YouTube for the first time in 2011, after a new government removed internet restrictions. Lifting my jaw off the floor, I nervously craned around the room to see if anyone would report me. No one did. They were all watching too.

Since then, the internet has become much more accessible. Nowadays, everybody has it on their phones. Prior to the 2021 coup, internet access was unrestricted. Since then, certain sites have been blocked again and internet activity is being monitored more. But I don't think we can ever totally go back to the pre-2011 dark ages. We have seen too many gigabytes of light to return there.

GETTING AROUND

Yangon's dizzying whirr of vehicles added another brick to my Great Wall of Contrasts. In my earliest memories, most people got around the old-fashioned way—walking or riding bicycles. My siblings and I stood in jealous awe the first time a neighbor rode into the village on a motorcycle. Before long another neighbor had one, then another. Soon these sleek, modern wonders were parked all over the village, arousing communal discontent. Then one momentous day, my dad rode up on a shiny, blue Kenbo motorcycle. I left my friends mid-game and ran straight home without saying goodbye. They didn't need an explanation though. I soon rode back past them like a new king in his chariot.

I probably wouldn't have held my head quite so high if I'd known how dinky our $300 Chinese motorcycle was compared to nicer ones abroad, but I didn't—and the moment was glorious. A few months later, the motorcycle broke and the glory faded. Ha! Imagine the quality of a new motorcycle that costs $300. Funny, right? That's why motorcycle repairmen have the highest job security in the country. Still, each repair was only pocket change, so my family rode and fixed the Kenbo on repeat until I moved to Yangon a couple of years later. I would have ridden a motorcycle in Yangon too, but it's not allowed. I considered riding a bicycle, but couldn't imagine safely squeezing through all the cars and people. Instead, I walked a lot and rode public transportation.

Only the wealthy elite own cars in Myanmar. The rest of us normal people get around Yangon in private taxis, pickup trucks, or buses. One taxi ride cost more than my daily wages back then, so I usually took pickup trucks or buses. These ran routes all over the city and only cost ten to thirty cents a ride. The pickup trucks had roofs over their beds, bench seats down both sides, and short plastic stools crammed in between. If the seats filled up, a few willing passengers stood on the back with the *spare*. The *spare* hung off his rear perch, barking out the next few stops through a wad of saliva and betel nut. He helped passengers on and off, collected fares, and made change from his photo-worthy bouquet of dirty bills. When pickups leave the city limits, passengers are allowed to sit on the roof. It's nice up there except for the hot sun. If you ever try it, make sure to hold the steel rail tightly and duck under low trees. I learned that the hard way.

Buses were the other affordable form of Yangon transportation. These dilapidated leftovers from other countries sported faded paint, smoky exhaust, and rusted-out holes. The engine compartment pumped hot air through the uninsulated floor panels, making the already scorching passenger cabin even more sauna-like. Rush hour on summer afternoons was the worst—even the window breeze felt hot.

I can still hear the bus's airbrakes releasing every few minutes as it jerked to a hurried stop. The *spare* hung from the side of the bus by one arm, rhythmically wooing waiting passengers with a list of upcoming destinations:

> *Hantha-waddy, Maha-myaing, Myay-ni-gone!*
> *Hantha-waddy, Maha-myaing, Myay-ni-gone!*
> *Myay-ni-gone!*

Then, the *spare* shoved boarding passengers, one by one, into the already full bus, which miraculously kept swallowing them without bursting. Inside, smelly strangers were smashed tight against each other on every side. No one moved without shoving and rubbing. Friends wisely warned me to watch my possessions. Women also had to watch for anonymous male hands.

At first, getting around the overcrowded city was an intimidating challenge. But like most of my other life contrasts, a big change eventually normalized and brought new perspective.

SARDINE CAN HOSTELS

The youth scene was bustling in my early Yangon days, especially in Hledan near the university. Hledan was filled with poor village kids like me who moved to the city with high hopes for the future. We all needed a few basic things, and Hledan had them all: cheap housing, cheap food, and cheap ways to learn job skills. Hledan was also centrally located, which meant cheaper bus fares. So I joined thousands of other youth from villages all over the country in calling Hledan's sardine can hostels home. In the backstreets, just blocks from Pyay Lan (the main north-south thoroughfare), thousands of dingy rooms offered budget lodging, perfect for my new home.

The large wooden structure was divided into a couple dozen small rooms, just big enough for two miniature plywood bed frames and three feet of walk space in between. That was it. The hostel provided nothing else—not even a foam mattress. The outdoor squatty potty was covered by wooden slats, and you often had to wait for a turn. Across the haphazard courtyard sat a concrete water tank and a small patch of concrete floor that we shared for showering and laundry. We drew water for both with a plastic bowl.

In the traditional Burmese way of showering, we don't take off all our clothes. Men shower in shorts, briefs, or a longyi. Women shower in a traditional wrap-around skirt. They pull the *tamain* higher than normal and tuck it under their armpits for modesty. This way of showering gets our clothes wet, but that's okay—they need washing too. We just hang them on the line to dry once we're done. Men shower with men and women with women. It's in the open and not weird for us, since we don't take off our clothes. Some hostels had different places for men and women to bathe, some just had different time slots. This wasn't much different from the village, except that here we were surrounded by tall buildings, and the sun only hit our little patch of earth for a few minutes a day. Sometimes, especially in rainy season, our clothes couldn't fully dry. But dry or not we had to take them off the line after a day to make room for others.

Looking back, I see two good things about Hledan's sardine can hostels. The first is obvious: they're cheap. Mine cost six dollars a month, and I couldn't have afforded much more. We transmigrated village kids didn't like everything about the hostels, but we couldn't have pursued our dreams without them. The hostels also gave us instant community with roommates and neighbors we didn't previously know, as we showered, hung laundry, and even waited in line for the toilet together. We didn't all become friends, but many of us did. We had all left our family and friends behind and needed people to joke and share meals with. The sardine cans gave us a good start on that.

MUTTON AND MONEY

Hledan was also bustling with budget rice shops, a perfect match for the hungry mass of youth migrants. The shop we visited most often sold three curries, a plate of rice, and a bowl of soup for less than one US dollar. And, believe it or not, the food was pretty good. Young fortune seekers packed around plastic tables *en masse* and made friends by sheer virtue of proximity. It was impossible to sit in one of these restaurants alone—even if you did come alone—which is something most of us never did anyway. When our friend group walked into the restaurant, under-aged waiters scrambled to pull over enough plastic chairs from wherever they had just been rearranged. Then we crammed in at a table with the strangers who were there first. Can you imagine sitting at a restaurant with your family, and six more guests bring chairs and shove in at your table? Welcome to Hledan's rice shops.

My favorite thing to eat at our regular rice shop was goat curry. I couldn't spare the thirty extra cents every day, but now and then I splurged on a few chunks of delicious, gravy-drowned goat meat to supplement my otherwise vegetarian "pile-and-eat" plate. I can still feel that warm, gravy-soaked rice grinding between my teeth, swishing over my tastebuds, and sliding down the back of my throat. I hope that shop is still open when I make it back for a visit.

The other thing Yangon's youth migrants needed—the most important of all—was jobs. But what kind of job is an unskilled village kid going to do in a bustling metropolis? Exactly. That's why cheap training schools taught accounting, computer skills, and English courses on every block. And while all these skills made their students more employable, English was king. More than any of the others, English opened a whole new world of possibilities to the fluent. Accounting and computing were quicker to learn, but without English, these jobs had a low ceiling on progress. English blew the roof off, offering international knowledge, international friendships, and international salaries. Good English might mean a tenfold pay raise. Jobs requiring English came with improved working conditions, elite social status, and a reputation boost for the family.

This is what drew us starry-eyed village kids to Yangon's city lights in the first place—not the sardine cans—but the dream of upward mobility and a chance to join the modern world. Did we want more money? Yes. But more than that, we were searching for broader horizons and the possibility of a better life. We didn't know if we'd succeed or not, but something deep inside urged us to give it a shot. Our country and our families had been in the dark for too long, choked by a repressive government and progress-impeding ideas. My generation had had enough. I had had enough. It was time to join the modern world or bust! So I packed into the sardine city and built my Wall of Life Contrasts brick by brick, far from family and many of our old ways, starving for something new—new jobs, new ideas, new fashions, and new music. The tide of change was rolling into Yangon on dilapidated buses, slow-motion internet cafes, and budget rice shops—all of these packed with a million village kid sardines. My generation was determined not to miss it. I was determined that *Tha Gyi's* family would not miss it, even if it took me far from home.

GOD SHOT

God is orchestrating unique opportunities through youth urbanization that he has uniquely gifted his people—including you—to leverage for the gospel at this moment in history.

> *Who knows, perhaps you have come to your royal position for such a time as this.* (Esth 4:14b)

PERSONAL REFLECTIONS

This is space to write personal discoveries, prayers, or anything else you find helpful. See this chapter's insights for mission in the back of the book or at jesusinthebuddhabelt.com.

14

New Friends, New Life

For eight or nine centuries now, the ancient city of Bagan's thousands of impressive temples have lured pious Buddhists on pilgrimage to upper Myanmar. In the old days, this arduous journey was often undertaken on foot. Today we use motorized vehicles, but the Burmese proverb remains: "A step a day, Bagan won't run away." Even if the journey to my dreams would be long, I was determined to reach it the same way ancient pilgrims reached the Buddhist holy site—by putting one foot in front of the other half a million times. Moving to Yangon was the first step. Signing up for the right training course was the second. Amassing enough English words and grammar structures to be fluent was steps three to five thousand. Half a million steps felt overwhelming, but I could always take the next single step. Then another. And another. I just had to keep moving forward. Practice, practice, practice. All this English practice led me to foreigners. Foreigners led me to church. And these two together led me to Jesus—the last person I expected to meet.

The journey to Jesus started when Ellen and Jill came to the restaurant where I worked. I was excited to practice English with two friendly foreigners, and they were excited to practice Burmese with me. Hours of language practice and laughter blossomed into friendship. Getting to know two cute foreign girls was fun and interesting—very interesting. Nearly everything about foreigners is different from Myanmar people. They have lighter skin, lighter hair, pointy noses, and different color eyes. Their clothes are different too. But what intrigued me most about Ellen and Jill was not their skin or nose shape, it was the look in their eyes and the expression on their faces.

The world was more peaceful and friendly with them in the room. When I spoke, Ellen and Jill listened like my words mattered. At first, I didn't know why these girls were so different from everyone else I knew. "It must be nice being so rich," I thought. "If I were a rich foreigner, I'd be like them too."

THEIR JESUS

As I got to know Ellen and Jill more, I could see that they weren't just different from Myanmar people, they were different from other foreigners too. Not all foreigners who came into the restaurant treated me like an important person. Most of them just politely talked to me when they wanted to buy something, then went on with more important things. Honestly, that's what I expected. Why would a rich foreigner treat a poor village kid like they mattered? I couldn't think of any reason. That's why Ellen and Jill took me off guard.

Eventually, I learned what made Ellen and Jill different—it was Jesus. I know because they told me. Ellen and Jill told me all kinds of things about Jesus—how he changed their lives, how he loved them, and how they loved him back. This was all strange to me, but not nearly as strange as the next thing they said: Jesus loved *me*. That was weird. I didn't know much about Jesus at that point, but I knew he was for foreigners—*not* for Burmese people. Burmese are Buddhist. Period. A Burmese worshipping Jesus is treason! We would have to betray our ethnic identity to do that. So I smiled and closed my ears when Ellen and Jill said the god of white foreigners loved me.

I was smiling on the outside, but frowning on the inside, as I remembered my people's history. If the god of white foreigners loved Burmese people, why did his British worshippers invade our country with guns? Did they desecrate our temples with boots and pillage our holy treasures because Jesus loved us? In my mind, becoming a Christian meant siding with the British—and I knew I did not want that.

Religion isn't something people can choose anyway. Ellen and Jill were born white American Christians; I was born a brown Burmese Buddhist. These things are determined by *karma* and ancestry, not by decisions. No, it's fine for white girls to talk about loving Jesus, but if they talk about *me* and Jesus ... I'll change the subject. I'm a Burmese Buddhist. My people already have a god. My mind is made up. I'll be friends with Ellen and Jill, but not with Jesus. Let's leave religion out of it.

A NEW GROUP OF FRIENDS

That's how I got started with Ellen, Jill, and Jesus—warmly open in one direction and frozen shut in the other. But things changed when they invited me to a free English class. One Saturday, I was off work and decided to check it out. Wow! There were so many students like me trying to learn English and make their way in the big city. A few foreigners also hung out with this group. They taught the class and led the practice circles. This class was different from my other English course. Here everybody was smiling and having fun—and it was contagious.

I started going to the free English class whenever I was off work. In the beginning, it was just another way to practice English, but it soon turned into a fun way to hang out with new friends. Most of the students in the free English class were Buddhist, but the ones I got to know best were Christian. Unlike Ellen and Jill, though, these people weren't born Christian. In fact, many of them were born Buddhist just like me. That was hard to understand. Foreigners worshipping Jesus made sense to me, but not Buddhist-born people. These Buddhist-born Christians were different than the other students, different than me and my sardine can hostel friends. They had something we were missing. I don't really know how to describe it. Lightheartedness? Peace? Joy? I'm not sure. Their lives weren't any easier than mine, but for them, the load didn't seem so heavy. A stream of cheerful optimism kept them afloat. I was interested.

TWO DIFFERENT WORLDS

Time and Yangon traffic rolled on. Every morning I woke at the sardine can hostel, splashed water on my face, and brushed my teeth at the shared water tank. I wound through Hledan's narrow alleys and crowded backstreets on foot and squished into the bed of a crowded pickup. Every evening after work, I rode the same pickup and walked the same narrow maze back to the shared water tank. Even though the hostel wasn't much, it was still good to be home at the end of the day. I stripped to my shorts and poured a few bowls of water over myself and the day's dirty laundry. Once my clothes and I were both lathered and rinsed, I hung the laundry on the line to dry. It was time to meet the other hungry sardine can dwellers at the rice shop. The same characters squished in each evening to eat, talk, and laugh at each other.

I kept going to the English class each Saturday and eventually accepted their invitation to try the Sunday church service. The church was run by the same people as the English class, and lots of students attended both. The preaching and some of the songs were in English, but they translated the sermon into Burmese. The church service was weird at first, but the people were nice. They slowly changed my perception of Christians. I didn't go to church to become a Christian. I mostly just went to practice English and see friends. Even if I did want to become a Christian, I was still Burmese. My family would never approve.

When church was over, a group of us made our way on foot to a roadside teashop near Sule Pagoda. I can still picture the scene in my mind. The sun had dipped behind most of the tall buildings by the time we got there. Only a splash of orange light remained, peeking through the cracks between buildings, painting warm patches on the street or sometimes on our faces. The teashop was outside and mobile. Ko Shwe and Ama Gyi prepared food and drinks from a metal cart with bicycle wheels. A few feet away, our group crowded around a knee-high plastic table and shared plates of Burmese salads, sprinkled with crushed peanuts and flanked by tiny spoons. Meanwhile, worn-out cars, jam-packed buses, and noisy pickups created a background hum a few yards away.

Burmese salads are not like salads I've seen from other countries. They start with a base ingredient, such as rice, tomato, ginger, chicken, etc. Then they mix in various combinations of peanut oil, bean powder, lime juice, crispy flat beans, sliced cabbage, tomato, dried shrimp, garlic, and roasted peanuts. Lots of Burmese salads are tasty, but *la-pet* is king of them all. The base ingredient in *la-pet* salad is pickled tea leaves. Ko Shwe and Ama Gyi made a good one that our group often enjoyed on Sunday afternoons. If you've ever tasted *la-pet* salad, your mouth is probably watering like mine right now. If you've never had it, maybe you can find a Burmese restaurant or Asian grocery store in your area and give it a try. Better yet, hop on a plane and try it on a miniature plastic stool near Sule! If I make it back there, I will treat you.

JESUS AT THE TEA SHOP

New friends, the Bible, and shared *la-pet* salad slowly led me into another realm of existence. I realized this one Sunday afternoon, looking around the teashop circle at my friends' faces. Their laughter and orange-tinted smiles swirled around me as the evening sun prepared to dip behind the skyline. I pictured Jesus in the circle with us, sitting on a miniature plastic stool, sharing *la-pet* salad with a tiny spoon. Inside, I felt peace and love. Wherever tomorrow took me, whether or not I achieved my life ambitions, I knew that everything was going to be okay. I could feel Jesus's smile The weight on my shoulders lifted.

No one else knew what happened in that moment. The noisy traffic kept buzzing by. My friends kept chatting and chewing. But to me, the familiar teashop scene looked totally different. In that moment, the Yangon sun was setting, but for me, it was just peeking over the horizon, chasing away the shadows and painting everything with beautiful orange light.

Was I a Christian now? I didn't know. I didn't like that word, but I didn't know how else to describe what was happening. I just knew something was different. The pastor often said Jesus was standing at the door knocking. "Jesus wants to come in and eat with us," he said, "but he won't do it unless we open the door and let him in." Maybe that's what happened that day in the tea shop—it must be. That day I opened the door to something new, to *someone* new—to Jesus—the man who surprisingly stood knocking on my Burmese Buddhist door. A few weeks later I made it official. Tha Gyi, the oldest son of Burmese Buddhist parents was now a baptized Christian.

GOD SHOT

God works in our lives through relational means—often using human to human relationships to deepen our relationship with him.

> *And let us consider one another in order to provoke love and good works, not neglecting to gather together, as some are in the habit of doing, but encouraging each other, and all the more as you see the day approaching.*
> (Heb 10:24–25)

PERSONAL REFLECTIONS

This is space to write personal discoveries, prayers, or anything else you find helpful. See this chapter's insights for mission in the back of the book or at jesusinthebuddhabelt.com.

15

Something Missing

A couple of years after meeting Jesus over *la-pet* salad, I was still going to English class, church, and the roadside tea shop. I was also still making my way back and forth to work, the sardine can hostel, and the rice joint. Slowly, these two disjointed worlds blurred the clarity of my first encounter with Jesus. I partly felt like a Christian with my friends at church, but I partly felt like a Buddhist with my friends in Hledan too. Neither place totally felt like home anymore. Questions came. Then doubts. Who was I? *What* was I? Buddhist or Christian? Burmese or something else?

Buddhist teachings randomly came to mind, and I didn't know what to do with them. The *Law of Impermanence*, for example, says nothing lasts. Things come, things go. They're here, then they're gone. This Buddhist teaching matched my experience. It was also useful in daily life. When my favorite shirt ripped or a friend moved away, the *Law of Impermanence* helped me cope with the loss. The pastor, on the other hand, taught *Permanence*—an eternal God and life that never ends. These two teachings didn't mesh. The *Law of Impermanence* made so much concrete sense that I couldn't deny it. But the Christian teaching on eternity was counterintuitive and hard to wrap my mind around.

The Buddha also taught that we are trapped in a never-ending cycle of death and rebirth. The goal of Buddhism is to escape this cycle. The pastor, on the other hand, said those who believe in Jesus will obtain the gift of never-ending life. Again, I was conflicted. Should I seek to escape the never-ending life cycle of Buddhism or seek to obtain the never-ending life offered by Jesus? In one case never-ending life is bad, in the other, it's supposed to be good. These ideas were at odds with each other too. The Buddha's teaching was like gravity and air to me—it naturally held me to the ground and filled my lungs without any conscious effort. Some of Jesus's teachings felt natural too, but some of them felt like bouncing on the moon and breathing with a spacesuit.

What was I to do? Could I accept the teaching of both Buddha and Jesus? I didn't know. The constant dissonance stirred me into confusion. Which teaching was true? Which god should I worship? And who had I become? Confusion turned to discouragement and discouragement to withdrawal. First, I started occasionally skipping the church service, then the free English class too. I told my friends I had to work or didn't feel well, but secretly, I just didn't want to go.

"Standing on two walls of the boat." I felt like a man in the Burmese proverb who tried to stand with his feet on opposing walls of a boat. It's precarious and hard to balance. You can't stay there for long, but you can't get off either. If you put your weight on one foot, the other side of the boat rises, threatening to tip the whole thing over. If you try to move the other way, the same thing happens in reverse. I didn't know how to escape this dilemma. Many days I wished I'd never gotten into it in the first place. My double life was exhausting.

WHICH HEAVEN?

One day a foreign friend asked me where Jesus would take me when I died. I replied in Burmese, *"Nat pyi."* He stared at me like the words didn't make sense. His puzzled look didn't make sense to me either. Christians say Jesus will take his followers to the abode of the sky (*kaung kin bone*) when they die. The Burmese call the abode of the sky *nat pyi* (abode of the *nats*). The Burmese word *nat* is similar to the English word for *angel* or *demon*: it can refer to either good or bad spiritual beings. Since the Christians said Jesus would take me to the *abode of the sky*, I logically concluded it was the same *nat pyi* I had known about my whole life. When my friend tried to clarify by asking the question again with the English word "*heaven*," I answered the same way: "*nat pyi.*"

Buddhism teaches *Thirty-One Abodes of Existence* in the never-ending cycle of rebirth and suffering. *Nat pyi* makes up six of these abodes and is much better than the lower abodes of hell, animals, and people. In fact, all kinds of pleasures exist there—but *nat pyi* is still inside the *Thirty-One Abodes of Existence*—and the dreaded cycle of rebirth and suffering. Since the goal of Buddhism is to escape all suffering, *nat pyi* is not our aim—*nirvana* is. Nirvana is obtained when suffering ceases. Suffering ceases when its root cause—desire—ceases. When a person ceases to desire, they cease to suffer—that's *nirvana*. It's like a candle that has been consumed by fire; it no longer exists. The Christians did not say Jesus would take me to *nirvana;* they said he would take me to the *abode of the sky*. So, naturally, I told my friend that Jesus would take me to *nat pyi* when I died. It was clear enough to me.

At this point, my puzzled friend realized that we had different ideas about *heaven*. "Jesus isn't going to take you to *nat pyi*," he explained. "The *heaven* Jesus promises is totally outside the *31 Abodes*, totally outside the cycle of rebirth, suffering, and desire. He continued, "Like *nirvana*, *heaven* has no old age, sickness, or death. But unlike *nirvana*, it's a real place. *Heaven* has houses, flowers, trees, and streets paved with gold. But most importantly, Jesus is there," he said. "Jesus will wipe away all our tears and live with us just like God lived with Adam and Eve in the Garden of Eden."

Wow! The heaven my friend talked about did *not* sound like *nat pyi* at all. But *nat pyi* is in the sky, so why did the Christians say Jesus would take his people to the *abode of the sky* (*kaung kin bone*) if that's not what they meant? Confusing! Who was I supposed to believe? Buddha, the pastor, or this foreign friend? How could I know who was right? I didn't even know where to start looking for answers. The more confused I became, the more I withdrew from my Christian friends. The sardine can community in Hledan was more comfortable. It felt like a refuge from the confusion. The people there understood me better—minus the Jesus part—but I wasn't so sure about that anymore. I was tired of standing with my feet on opposite sides of the boat. But I didn't know how to get off either.

STRUGGLE AND CHANGE

I tried to forget the confusion by busying myself with work. But many things at work reminded me of Ellen and Jill. I wondered how they were doing back in their country. The other foreign friend sometimes visited me, but that wasn't much help either. He didn't understand what I was going through. It was easy for foreigners. They followed the way of their family, the way of their country—the way the current was carrying them. I was swimming upstream. It was exhausting and I didn't want to do it anymore. True, I had an encounter with Jesus, but the memory of that moment was fading farther into the past.

Things went on this way for a while. I hadn't completely left Jesus. I still had good feelings toward him and even talked to him sometimes. But the further I grew from my Christian friends, the closer I returned to my Buddhist roots. All the while, I kept learning English, looking for opportunities, and applying for positions abroad. Then, one fateful day, just before hope disappeared over the horizon, I got a job offer! *Nat pyi* at last! I could hardly believe it!

The next two weeks busily blurred by as I gathered official documents, filled out forms, and exchanged wishes with family and friends. Goodbye, Hledan sardine era. Hello, new life abroad! And just like that, with hope and my first plane ride, I landed on the Singapore tarmac. It seemed too good to be true. Was this really happening to a Burmese village boy? I could hardly wait for what came next.

HOMESICK IN SINGAPORE

Singapore and Yangon are perfect antonyms: dark and light, day and night, bitter and sweet. Seriously, Singapore is sparkly clean—Yangon, dilapidated and littered. Singapore's old buildings still look new. Yangon's new buildings already look old. In Singapore, people cross the street at crosswalks when the light says go. In Yangon, crowds shove across the street one lane at a time in whatever location they please, forcing the cars to stop. Spitting betel nut juice in Singapore will get you fined. In Yangon, you are lucky if no one spits betel on you. Each Singaporean road, lawn, and grocery display is perfectly designed. In Yangon they are haphazard and out of place. Two cities could not be more different. My Great Wall of Contrasts was growing.

Each morning at 7:20 a.m., I walked fifteen minutes to the MRT station, rode the train for ten minutes, then walked five more minutes to get to work. I carefully observed each shopping mall, grocery store, and high rise in the beginning. But after a dozen or so trips there and back, the sparkly new city jolted my senses less. It still felt nothing like Myanmar, of course, but I was slowly adapting—adapting on one hand *and* growing homesick on the other. Then, one day, I discovered a hidden respite. From outside, this building looked like the rest, but a world of surprises waited behind its unassuming doors. First, a familiar Lay Phyu melody hit my ears. Then, I saw the letters. Not English letters. Not Chinese letters. But those wonderful, circular ones I had learned in school. I saw them first on a newspaper, then on some books, then on handwritten signs advertising each shop's special items—all in my own wonderful language! I flashed back to those first days learning the Burmese alphabet: "Ka-gyi, kha-kwe, ga-nge, ga-gyi, nga ... " A crowded room of green and white-clad kindergarteners echo the teacher in unison. I proudly chant along until Dad picks me up at the end of the day. What innocent times those were. I couldn't help but crack a smile.

Then, a flurry of familiar smells snapped my homesick nostrils back from the childhood schoolhouse to the present moment in downtown Singapore. First *mohinga*, then beef and potato curry, then my favorite—*la-pet* salad! One by one, these savory smells beckoned me home. I couldn't fit enough of the newfound treasures into my stomach that day, but I packed in as much as I could and topped it off with a steamy cup of Burmese tea. *"Cho saint!"* I yelled my order to the tea master. Two minutes later a sweet, creamy treasure arrived at my table, along with a tiny stirring spoon—the same type of spoon we ate *la-pet* salad with after church on Sundays. I swirled the spoon around in the cup a few times, carefully scraping the sweetened condensed milk off the bottom. Then, I dropped the spoon on the saucer, grabbed the cup handle, and slowly lifted it to my lips. That sweet, savory sip of tea brought back a flood of warm feelings that made this foreign place feel friendly for the first time.

LONGING FOR HOME

I can't describe the good that little piece of Myanmar in Singapore did for me. If you've ever visited a foreign country, you can relate. Maybe it was even more meaningful because I had already felt far from home for so long—even before leaving my country. The smells and tastes of home I discovered inside that secret Burmese portal, didn't clear up all my confusion about life. But they did make me feel more grounded, more connected—to myself, my people, and my past. And that made things more bearable.

Will I ever go back to Myanmar? Definitely! But not until saving enough money to make a decent life there. In the meantime, I send money to my parents and siblings, live frugally, and save as much as I can each month. Singapore isn't home, but it gives me a chance to make home better—for my family who's still there—and hopefully for me too one day in the future.

UNANSWERED QUESTIONS

Meanwhile, my questions remain unanswered. Am I a Christian or a Buddhist? No. Yes. Which one do you mean? I still don't know how to make sense of the contradictions. I guess I'm still precariously standing with one foot on either side of the boat. I don't go to church anymore, but I still know Jesus is out there, and I think he hears my prayers. One day, I hope to sort it out better—maybe when I get back home.

There is one question that I *have* been able to answer though. I know for sure that I am Burmese. Beyond that, I don't know much. I have always been told that Burmese equals Buddhist. But after struggling with my identity these past ten years, I'm not sure that equation works anymore. I know I am still Burmese. But what does it mean to be Buddhist? Does it mean I was born into a certain family and have the teaching imprinted on my subconscious? Does it mean I believe and practice the Buddha's teaching? How about bowing down and praying to statues and monks? Can some of these things be true without the others? And can a Buddhist believe in Jesus? I'm more and more convinced that the equation is not as simple as I was taught. Maybe I can be one variable without being the other.

I also wonder, "What is a Christian?" Is it someone from a Western country or a Myanmar ethnic minority? Were Christians born that way, or does it involve a decision? Are they Christians if they go to church but don't practice the teaching? Can Christians believe any of the Buddha's teachings, or do they have to reject it all? The lines aren't as clear as they used to be on either side of my Great Wall of Contrasts. I think that's why I don't know how to answer my own question, and I'm still precariously straddling the boat, waiting for someone to help me. In the meantime, I need to make some money. And after that, I hope to go home.

In God's wisdom, he has not only commanded his people to share the gospel, but also to make robust disciples, teaching those who believe to practice everything he commanded (Matthew 28:18–20).

GOD SHOT

In God's wisdom, he has not only commanded his people to share the gospel, but also to make robust disciples, teaching those who believe to practice everything he commanded.

> Jesus came near and said to them, "All authority has been given to me in heaven and on earth. Go, therefore, and make disciples of all nations, baptizing them in the name of the Father and of the Son and of the Holy Spirit, teaching them to observe everything I have commanded you. And remember, I am with you always, to the end of the age."
>
> (Matt 28:18–20)

PERSONAL REFLECTIONS

This is space to write personal discoveries, prayers, or anything else you find helpful. See this chapter's insights for mission in the back of the book or at jesusinthebuddhabelt.com.

16
Going Deeper: Repainting the White Colonialist Jesus

Close your eyes and picture Jesus. What do you see? Seriously, pause for a second and try it. What color is his skin? Hair? Eyes? Does he look like a relative or a strange man from a distant country? I've never seen Jesus and don't know anyone who has. But I still had a vivid mental image of him when Ellen and Jill first mentioned his name. Of course, that image has changed since I've come to know Jesus, but I think many Burmese people still see Jesus how I used to. This mental image is probably a lot different than yours and makes it harder—not easier—for us to come to Jesus. Would you like to know what we see when you say his name?

Jesus has white skin. That's the first thing we see. He's a white man with a pointy nose—not brown and flat-nosed like us. This is strange because there aren't many pointy-nosed white people in our country. I had only seen them on TV before moving to the big city. Pointy-nosed white people are foreigners who worship Jesus. Two hundred years ago, white Jesus worshippers from Great Britain visited our country. They came with Indian soldiers, cannon balls, and long-barreled rifles. They brought Jesus too.

The British Christians weren't happy to stay in their own country. So they came to ours—not as friendly guests—but as uninvited enemies. They came not to listen, but to speak; not to give, but to take; not to honor, but to desecrate. The British Christians came to steal our land, subjugate our people, and get rich off our natural resources. After years of vandalism, theft, killing, and profiteering they succeeded in making Burma a

British colony. That's where our beef with Jesus begins. We see him as a white man, worshipped by white people—god of the British—who pillaged our country and plundered our freedom.

The British changed many things about our country, including the architectural landscape. They built massive edifices for government administration, clock towers for timekeeping, parks and memorials for their revered generals. They built some good things too, like roads, hospitals, and schools, but these benefits do not excuse their many sins. Since the British worshipped Jesus, they also built churches. I know these things from riding around Yangon's historic downtown. Many of the buildings remain, serving as a forceful reminder of how the white conquerors came to us propelled by three M's: merchant, military, and mission. These three forces motivated the colonial British to dock their boats, hoist their canons, and raise their cathedrals in our country—against our people's will. This is part of the mental image many Burmese have of Jesus.

GOD OF THE WHITE INDIANS

The British weren't the only white men to visit our country, but to us, they're all the same. They all have white skin and pointy noses, they all speak English, and they all worship Jesus. To us, they are all *Kala Phyu*, a term coined by one of the ancient Burmese kings. *Kala* is what we call Indians. *Phyu* is the Burmese word for white. Put them together and you get *Kala Phyu*, White Indians. This term provides a meaningful description of white people for a few reasons. First, the British and the Indians came to our country together. The British colonized India before Burma and brought many Indians with them, first as soldiers and later as government staff.

We also call white people *Kala Phyu* because their facial features look like Indians. Of course, Indians are darker than white men, but to us flat-nosed Burmans, their facial features share a strong resemblance. Look at their noses, jawlines, foreheads, and chins. They are nothing like our people and a lot like each other. *Kalas* also typically wear long beards. White men are sometimes clean-shaven, but their *Kala* beards sprout the moment they put down the razor. Burmese men (along with most other men from our country) can't grow much facial hair. The only people we see with facial hair are Indians and white men: two types of *Kala*. Paintings show Jesus with a *Kala* beard too. This makes him look like a foreign, unfriendly *Kala Pyu Paya*, God of the White Indians.

The term *Kala Phyu* also communicates our historical association with white people. Many Burmese disdain—if not outright hate—Indian *Kalas*. There are historical, cultural, economic, and religious reasons for all of this. As far as I know, the Burmese have never liked the *Kala*. Many times in our history—even recently—there has been violence between the two groups. In the 1960s the Burmese-dominated military junta forced many *Kalas* to leave the country and go back to their homeland. Many Burmese still want the *Kalas* to leave, and some of us have a similar emotion toward the white colonialists in our history books. Sure, Burma was better off under Colonial rule than it has been since, but the sins of Colonialism still affect many Burmese people's view of Jesus. For us, Jesus is by default a *Kala Pyu Paya*.

AMERICANS AND MINORITIES

American *Kala Phyus* have also visited our country in significant numbers. Americans brought Bibles to Burma before the British brought guns. But to us, the British and Americans were all the same—just different strands on the white man's 3M rope (merchant, military, mission). Adoniram Judson was among the first Americans to call Burma home. He compiled the first Burmese-English dictionary and translated the Bible into Burmese in the first half of the nineteenth century. Through his work, and those who followed him, large numbers from the Karen, Kachin, and Chin tribes became Christian. These ethnic minority groups were not Buddhist though—they were animist. Among the Burmese Buddhist majority Judson and his colleagues saw very little fruit.

Why did the animistic minority groups respond differently to the message of Jesus than the Burmese did? When American missionaries first came, these people were backward village dwellers with only oral traditions and no form of writing. Their spirit worship included powerful invisible beings and animal sacrifices. This made it easy for them to accept Jesus as the miracle-working final sacrifice who appeased the invisible God. The missionaries reduced these groups' languages to writing, taught them to read the Bible, and provided them with an education for which they are forever grateful. Some of these groups have been so thoroughly Christianized that Jesus is now just as much a part of their ethnic identity as Buddha is for the Burmese. They love their white missionary heroes! The Burmese, on the other hand, have quite a different view because of our different history.

In the Burmese view, Christianized minority groups were seen as poor, misguided folk who submitted to the white man's culture and religion. They received a lot of material benefits from their conversion and continue to enjoy the fruits of it today. However, many Burmese believe these groups only converted because the Buddha's teaching didn't reach them first. If the minority groups had already been enlightened by the true teaching of Buddha, why would they ever trade it for a foreign culture and god? The Burmese see Jesus as a foreigner who is worshipped by foreign, white people—people who don't wear longyis, don't show reverence, and don't take off their shoes at the proper time. Adopting these lesser ways is considered disgraceful. That's what is swimming in the Burmese subconscious when you tell us about Jesus. Does that affect your approach?

A NEW AND BETTER IMAGE

It took a lot of relearning and new experiences, but my original mental image of Jesus has changed. Nowadays when I close my eyes, I see him with brown skin, like mine. I see him wearing a longyi, like mine. I hear him speaking Burmese words, like mine. I know Jesus was from Nazareth and looked like the people of his day, but I can't help but think he would wear a longyi and shave his face if he visited Myanmar. I picture Jesus squeezing into a crowded Yangon bus, sleeping in a sardine can hostel, drinking a cup of *cho saint* at a roadside teashop, and sharing Burmese salads with a tiny spoon. I see him with friends—laughing, listening, explaining things—that's what he'd be doing.

I have learned that Jesus isn't a *Kala Phyu*. He's not British, American, or Kachin. Jesus is a Jewish man from the Middle East. The pastor once said, "Jesus splits the East-West divide down the middle of the map. He was born in the middle of the map. He healed the sick with compassion and taught the common folk wisdom in the middle of the map. And he was nailed on a cross in the middle of the map, with his arms stretched out in both directions—to the East and the West—calling us all to salvation and a new way of life."

That's the Jesus I want my people to close their eyes and see. That's the Jesus they need. That's the Jesus *I* need! But that's not the Jesus who's been most often portrayed in our history. Foreigners and ethnic minorities have painted a different picture. That picture is compelling us in the wrong direction. It's confusing and encumbered by cultural imperialism. I want my people to see the real Jesus when they close their eyes, but how is that going to happen until one of his people—from the East, the West, or anywhere in between—comes and paints a new, more accurate picture?

This is unlikely to result in instant gratification. It took centuries to shape our current mental canvas of Jesus. Repainting will require a patient hand, but isn't that how masterpieces are made? I don't think many of my people will come to Jesus unless someone does this for them. Those who pick up the brush to attempt this difficult task will have a much greater chance of success if they sit with us at the teashop, grab a cup of *cho saint*, and share *la-pet* salad with a tiny spoon.

GOD SHOT

Jesus stripped himself of every divine privilege and became like us in every way, so that he could make atonement for our sins, relate to our difficulties, and bring us to God as a merciful and faithful high priest.

> *Therefore, he had to be like his brothers and sisters in every way, so that he could become a merciful and faithful high priest in matters pertaining to God, to make atonement for the sins of the people. For since he himself has suffered when he was tempted, he is able to help those who are tempted.*
> (Heb 2:17–18)

PERSONAL REFLECTIONS

This is space to write personal discoveries, prayers, or anything else you find helpful. See this chapter's insights for mission in the back of the book or at jesusinthebuddhabelt.com.

DISCUSSION AND PRAYER GUIDE

This was the final chapter in Tha Gyi's story. See the Discussion and Prayer Guide in the back of this book for deeper personal or group reflection or scan the QR code for an online version.

jesusinthebuddhabelt.com
Also scan this QR code to:

SHARE your thoughts or ask a question

EXPLORE the topics of this book further with free articles, photos, videos, and recipes

CONNECT with ongoing mission initiatives in the Buddha Belt

Epilogue: Our New Friends Now and Where We Go From Here

We have sat across the table from our new friends for sixteen chapters now. Through their stories, we have crossed the ocean and traveled in time to see both the glory of God and the mess of humanity in new and challenging ways. We have discovered a great surprise—Jesus at work in the Buddha Belt, and, hopefully, we have received some new light along the way. Now, how might we bring Aung, Bawi, Lin, and Tha Gyi's stories to a satisfying end? And, if you may graciously humor me (speaking as the author now) for a few short seconds, what might each of us do with the light we've received from their stories?

Let's consider our friends first. At present, Aung is pastoring a small church of Ta'ang believers and helping translate the Bible into their language. His children, including the one who was saved by a last-ditch prayer to Jesus, are grown and serving the Lord. Bawi still lives in Banyan Ridge, shepherding the flock he started, and raising three beautiful children with Sky. His hairline is receding, but not his energy level. Sky is still smiling and making delicious food for everyone. Lin married a sweet Christian girl from another ethnic group, and they are serving as missionaries together in upper Myanmar. He has escaped the dangers of singleness and found a great ministry partner for life! Tha Gyi? Sadly, I can't find any way to contact him. His story's ending is unknown, just like 180 million others in the Buddha Belt, the vast majority of whom are still considered unreached by the gospel. These millions of fellow humans have not yet encountered the real Jesus and are distressed about their personal and collective futures due to the chaotic environment around them.

That brings us to our second question: what will you and I do with the light we've received from our new friends' stories? First, if you have made it through this book and do not yet know Jesus in a personal way, our new friends and I wholeheartedly commend him to you. We have found him to be a dear friend, a strong help, a wise guide, a savior, and so much more. Jesus welcomes all of us, for the first time or the hundredth time, "Come to me, all of you who are weary and carry heavy burdens, and I will give you rest." You can find Jesus in prayer, the Bible, and a community of sincere Christians. If you need help with that, send us a message.

Second, right now, millions in Myanmar and across the Buddha Belt are disillusioned with life and religion. Their normal unquestioning conformism has been cracked, and they are willing to consider different alternatives in unprecedented numbers. This is a historic window of opportunity, but it may not last long. As we said in the beginning, the soul of Myanmar—along with many of its neighbors across the Buddha Belt—is hanging in the balance. Good or evil, God or the devil, the spirit of Lincoln or the spirit of Hitler—which will prevail? The answer may, at least partly, depend on what you and I do when we put down this book. Might you be willing to consider how your prayers, passions, skills, and resources could influence the people of the Buddha Belt's outcome in a positive direction? If so, please visit jesusinthebuddhabelt.com to learn how you can help others like Aung, Bawi, Lin, and Tha Gyi find the surprising answer they are desperately longing for—the only true hope of salvation, wherever we live—Jesus, Lord and Savior, unexpectedly at work right in the heart of the Buddha Belt.

WE'D LOVE TO HEAR FROM YOU

Email our team to learn specific ways you can make a difference in the Buddha Belt, to let us know how God has used this book in your life, or anything else you'd like to share: **contact@jesusinthebuddhabelt.com**

Thank you so much for reading this book! If you haven't already ...

CLAIM YOUR FREE GIFT BUNDLE NOW

jesusinthebuddhabelt.com/gift

Scan the QR code or enter the URL above to download a free gift bundle, including an exclusive bonus chapter and a high-resolution prayer map of the Buddha Belt.

PRAYER RESOURCES

jesusinthebuddhabelt.com/pray
Scan or enter URL for more free prayer resources.

Appendix 1
Discussion and Prayer Guide

AUNG'S STORY
(Chapters 1–4)

 REFLECTION QUESTIONS

1. Aung decided to leave Buddhism and follow Jesus after realizing he couldn't follow all the rules of his religion and experiencing a powerful answer to prayer. If you are a follower of Jesus, how did you make that decision? If you're not a follower of Jesus yet, what is holding you back? Compare and contrast your journey with Aung's.

2. Aung faced a lot of persecution after becoming a follower of Jesus, but instead of turning back to Buddhism, the persecution helped strengthen his faith. Reflect on a time you have faced persecution for your faith. How did it affect you?

3. What are the pros and cons of Thant asking the village leader's permission before sharing the gospel in a new village? Do you agree or disagree with this strategy? Explain.

4. What could you use from Aung's personal experience or the analogies he shared (drowning man, tote-see-doe children's game, his brother's funeral) to more effectively tell others about Jesus?

5. What resonated with you from Aung's story and what do you think God might want you to do in response?

PRAYER POINTS

Fast Fact: The nation of Myanmar has a population of 58 million people and 52 people groups that are considered unreached by the gospel. Among these Unreached People Groups are three subgroups of Ta'ang with a combined population of over 1 million.

1. Pray for Aung and Thant and the other workers who are sharing the good news in Myanmar. Here are a few prayer ideas to get started with:

   - A deep, abiding connection with God (John 15:1–11)
   - Boldness and clarity to powerfully share the gospel (Eph 6:19–20)
   - That the gospel will spread rapidly and be honored (2 Thess 3:1)
   - Perseverance to make disciples (Matt 28:19–20)
   - Wisdom and innocence for living in an environment that is hostile to the gospel (Matt 10:16–20)
   - Protection from those who oppose the gospel (2 Thess 3:2)

2. Read Matthew 9:35–38. Ask God to send more workers like Aung and Thant to share the good news with the Ta'ang and other Unreached People Groups of Myanmar.

BAWI'S STORY
(Chapters 5–8)

 REFLECTION QUESTIONS

1. The Christian community Bawi grew up in, ironically, praised the missionaries from their history, but showed no interest in telling their Buddhist neighbors about Jesus. Is your faith community's interest in sharing the gospel similar or different from Bawi's? What are some reasons for this?

2. When Bawi truly came to know God, he became passionate about sharing the good news of Jesus—often even weeping for the lost in prayer. Why do you think that is?
Have you ever had a similar experience? Explain.

3. Later on, Bawi lost his zeal and obedience to share the good news. Recall a time that you have strayed from doing what you know God wants. What are some reasons we struggle with this? And what can get us back on track with God?

4. Is there anything that you know God wants you to do that you are holding back on right now? If so, what's keeping you from doing what God wants?

5. Bawi took the humble posture of a language, culture, and religion learner in his early days in Flower village. What fruit did that bear? And how might this approach help us share the good news of Jesus?

6. Just as Bawi was gaining friends and fluency in the local language, the neighboring village made a push to force him out. Should Christians who share the gospel expect this kind of persecution or should Bawi have done something different to avoid this? Compare with the missionary journeys in Acts chapters 13–21 and 2 Timothy 3:10–12.

7. Bawi did not see as many people in Banyan Ridge come to know Jesus as he wanted. What do you think the reasons for this were? How would you counsel a brother or sister who shared this struggle?

8. What did you learn from Bawi's story that could help you more effectively communicate the good news of Jesus with people that are different from you?

 PRAYER POINTS

Fast Fact: There are an estimated 1.5 million Chin people in Myanmar, including 53 sub-tribes. Chin people, like Bawi, make up a large percentage of the Myanmar nationals serving as pastors and missionaries.

1. Pray for good news work in Myanmar by Bawi and others. See Prayer Point #1 from Aung's Story above for specific items.

2. Ask God to reveal five people in your life who need to know Jesus. Write their names down and begin praying for them regularly.

LIN'S STORY
(Chapters 9–12)

 REFLECTION QUESTIONS

1. What are some challenges to the Myanmar mission context that Lin's story reveals? Do you think it's helpful to know about these dangers or not? Explain.

2. Why are people from other countries particularly vulnerable to the dangers discussed above?

3. How can people from outside of Myanmar successfully mitigate some of these dangers in their Myanmar mission efforts? Be specific.

4. How do you feel about Lin's examples of using Buddhist teachings to point people to Jesus? Is this helpful or dangerous? Explain.

5. Do pastors that you admire use illustrations and cultural allusions to communicate God's truth more clearly? How is this similar or different from Lin's use of Buddhist teachings as bridges to Jesus?
6. How has what you have learned from this book changed how you would approach a Buddhist with the gospel?
7. Are there any applications for sharing the gospel with your non-Christian neighbors even if they are not Buddhist? Explain.

 PRAYER POINTS

Fast Fact: Over 31 million of Myanmar's 58 million citizens are ethnically Burmese. According to joshuaproject.net, only 0.08 percent of Burmese people are Christian. Many Burmese villages have no churches and no Christian witness.

1. Pray that Lin and the small number of other Burmese believers will be mature, unashamed disciples who boldly honor Jesus with their words and deeds (Rom 1:14–17; Matt 5:13–16).
2. Pray for Lin and the other Burmese Christians who are sharing the gospel. See Prayer Point #1 from Aung's Story above for specific items.
3. Pray for the five people listed in prayer point #2 from Bawi's story above. Ask God to reveal their need for him and the greatness of Jesus. Pray for an opportunity to talk to them and that they will be receptive.

THA GYI'S STORY
(Chapters 13–16)

 REFLECTION QUESTIONS

1. Tha Gyi left his family, friends, and rural village to seek a better life in Myanmar's biggest city. How did this move make him more open to Jesus than he was before?

2. Thousands of young people like Tha Gyi are moving to cities from rural villages. They are often more open to new ideas and free from social pressures than people living in villages. What are some ways this massive opportunity can be maximized for the gospel?

3. What role did foreigners play in Tha Gyi's faith journey? What were the benefits and limitations of this?

4. Tha Gyi's struggle to reconcile old Buddhist beliefs with his new faith in Jesus led to confusion and disillusionment. Consider his misunderstanding about heaven as one example of this. How did the Christians in Tha Gyi's life contribute to this problem? What could they have done to avoid or correct this?

5. How do you think Tha Gyi's lack of deep discipleship contributed to his struggle and confusion? What kind of discipleship process and content would be optimal for growing healthy new believers from a Buddhist background?

6. How does understanding the Burmese view of Jesus as a *Kala Pyu Paya* and a White Colonialist make you feel? What important implications does this have for communicating the good news? What mistakes might we make without understanding this?

PRAYER POINTS

Fast Fact: Countless thousands of Burmese and other Unreached People Groups are migrating to cities in Myanmar and abroad each year. These urban youth migrants often have increased receptivity to new ideas, including the gospel. Foreigners and Myanmar nationals can partner with prayerful strategies and deep discipleship to maximize this amazing gospel opportunity.

1. Pray for Tha Gyi and other Buddhist background believers to effectively reconcile their past beliefs with their new faith and identity in Jesus.

2. Pray for Christians reaching out to Myanmar Buddhists (and other faiths) to establish new believers with an intentional process for deep discipleship.

3. Pray for effective partnerships between foreigners and Myanmar nationals to fulfill the Great Commission among Myanmar's remaining Unreached People Groups.

OUR NEW FRIENDS NOW AND WHERE WE GO FROM HERE

(Epilogue)

 REFLECTION QUESTIONS

1. What are your key takeaways from this book?
2. Is there anything that you feel God wants you to do in response? What is your next step forward?

 PRAYER POINTS

Fast Fact: At the time of this writing, joshuaproject.net says 46 million fellow humans in Myanmar and 3.4 billion worldwide have little or no access to the gospel. These overwhelming numbers can freeze us with discouragement. But instead of getting lost in millions and billions (that's God's job), let's focus on taking whatever simple step lies in front of us and leaving the results to him.

1. Ask God to show you what specific action(s) he wants you to take in response to this book. Write your impressions.

2. Share this with someone and pray together for help in following through. Set a time for checking in (if that's helpful).

SCAN FOR WAYS TO GET INVOLVED.

jesusinthebuddhabelt.com/getinvolved

If you haven't already, please let us know if this book has helped you in any way or you have taken any action step in response. Scan the QR code above and click contact or email **contact@jesusinthebuddhabelt.com.**

Appendix 2
Insights for Mission

FREE PDF DOWNLOAD

jesusinthebuddhabelt.com/insightspdf

Scan or enter the URL to download a free Insights for Mission PDF.

AUNG'S STORY

Unexpected Answer

For the last two centuries, the Buddha Belt has been highly resistant to the gospel, but Aung's story includes several elements that can help lead Buddhists to Jesus.

- Realizing the impossibility of keeping the Buddhist Law is helping some Buddhists see their sin and need for a Savior.
- In the face of problems beyond their ability, some Buddhists are trying prayer to Jesus—and receiving answers.
- Many times, after receiving answers from prayer to Jesus, Buddhists are eager to learn more about him and his ways.

Divorce or Miracle?

This part of Aung's story shows us some keys to helping new believers grow.

- Most new believers in the Buddha Belt face intentional persecution for following Jesus, but through their perseverance in faith, God strengthens them and validates their gospel witness.

- Buddhist background believers in Jesus may not know many Christians or many Bible verses at conversion, but they desperately need the encouragement of Christian community and the Bible to withstand persecution and grow mature.

Thant and the Crazy Christians

This chapter reveals some of the reasons new believers are persecuted in the Buddha Belt.

- Preexisting wrong ideas about Jesus and conflicting ideas from Buddhism skew many Buddhist's perceptions of the good news.
- Many people across the Buddha Belt do not believe they can choose their religion any more than they can choose their ethnicity—for them, both are something inherited that they cannot change.
- Persecution is a normal, often unavoidable, experience for new believers in the Buddha Belt and is intensified by the communal nature of their societies.
- Powerful, tangible evidence of God's love and power leads some Buddhists to Jesus, but many who see this still choose to oppose him.

Going Deeper: Trail Guides to Jesus

In this chapter Aung reminds us of the need to share the good news and some tools to help.

- Many unreached people groups across the Buddha Belt have very few Christians and little or no access to the gospel. This changed for Aung—and will only change for others—when Christians are willing to guide the unreached to the path of Jesus (Rom 10:13–15).
- Historically, most Buddhists have been highly resistant to the gospel, but across the Buddha Belt some, like Aung, are coming to Jesus by experiencing his power through prayer along with an explanation of the gospel that meaningfully communicates with Buddhists.
- Understanding that they cannot keep the Laws of Buddhism can show Buddhists that they need a savior, and analogies from their existing worldview can help them understand that the savior is Jesus.

BAWI'S STORY

Awakening

In this chapter Bawi shows us the sad state of many traditional churches and the profound change that encountering God can make.

- When Christians do not have a deep experience of Jesus and a vivid memory of the gospel's work in their own lives, they are likely be more concerned with interchurch and worldly affairs than with sharing the gospel with unbelievers.
- A fresh encounter with God (or possibly initial conversion) can rescue Christians from this sad condition and ignite us with a passion to share the gospel.

Village Fire

In this chapter Bawi begins a new mission among an unreached people group in Banyan Ridge. His struggles and perseverance teach some helpful principles.

- Geographical, linguistic, cultural, and other barriers present significant challenges to getting the gospel to the remaining unreached people groups. But God wants his people to overcome these barriers for his glory and the good of the unreached.
- Long-term missionaries will have to give up some of their comforts and make a significant investment in learning a new language and way of life, earning local people's trust, and making friends, etc. to have a successful mission among the unreached.
- Sharing the gospel among the unreached often comes with persecution for the missionaries. Rather than doubting themselves and feeling discouraged, missionaries should rejoice and prayerfully persevere, realizing this is a normal part of how the gospel has been advancing from the beginning and that God will defend their cause. (Matt 5:1–12)

Love and Blindfolds

This chapter introduces Sky, who becomes Bawi's wife, and her journey to Jesus. Bawi also reflects on the fruit of his labor in Banyan Ridge, offering helpful perspective and insight.

- In the Buddha Belt, and elsewhere, unbelievers carefully watch Christians and form opinions of God based on their behavior. When Christians abuse God's grace with sinful lifestyles, we make the gospel look foolish to unbelievers. Conversely, when Christians let the light of our good deeds shine before men, people will give glory to our father in heaven (Matt 5:16).
- Dreams are a powerful way that God speaks to some in the Buddhist world. We can pray for God to give Buddhists meaningful dreams, ask if they have had dreams, and prayerfully help them understand their meanings.
- We want to see the gospel spread fast and far, but it often moves at a tortoise pace instead. And while we should be willing to evaluate our methods, we should also be willing to listen to God and remain faithful even if the fruit is less than we hope for. Faithful obedience is a better measure of success than the number of converts. (Remember the prophets.)

Going Deeper: Becoming Like a Buddhist (to Win Some to Jesus)

In this chapter Bawi models three additional principles for communicating the gospel cross-culturally.

- The long, hard work of learning the local language, culture, and religion is essential to helping outsiders avoid unnecessary offenses and build bridges of understanding for the gospel.
- Building bridges from a host culture's previous knowledge can help increase understanding and minimize barriers to the gospel—but it cannot produce conversion.
- The Burmese proverb, "Friendly with the person; friendly with the teaching," highlights the important role of relationships across the Buddha Belt in increasing people's openness to new ideas, including the gospel.

LIN'S STORY

Adoption

In this chapter, Lin's story sheds light on racial issues hindering the mission and how he personally overcame them. Pastor Kyaw's example also shows the importance of following up with new believers with ongoing discipleship.

- Entrenched racism among different ethnic groups can be a major hindrance to God's mission, but also presents an opportunity for the gospel to shine brightly—doing it's unique work of breaking down racial barriers and creating one new family in God. (Gal 3:28–29; Eph 2:11–22)

- Exposure to different ethnic groups can also reduce negative stereotypes and feelings toward other races. Listening to, learning from, and making friends with them is helpful in overcoming racism and in effectively communicating the gospel.

- Good shepherds do not abandon new believers after initial conversion, but faithfully follow up with ongoing discipleship to help them establish deep roots and grow mature.

Murder Plot

In this chapter Lin shows us some challenges and pitfalls to avoid in mission work.

- Unmarried missionaries have some advantages but also face unique struggles and vulnerabilities that can severely damage the mission. Those sending missionaries, and the missionaries themselves, should find wise ways to mitigate these dangers to the missionaries and the mission.

- Donating money is one of the easiest ways for foreigners to feel like they're making a difference—and the things money buys can boost the mission—but foreigners donating lots of money to poor local people without sufficient relationship and accountability pose major risks to the donors, the recipients, and Christ's reputation.

- Many times, the flow of money donated for mission is tied to statistical reports of people who heard the gospel, baptisms, etc. These reports alone are not a reliable measure of mission success as they can be tempting and easy to manipulate or misrepresent.

Inside Addiction

This chapter adds to the conversation about crossing cultures with the gospel and exposes the problem of drug addiction that is rampant in parts of the Buddha Belt and the dangers it poses to mission.

- The gospel moves into people's lives through layers of race, culture, relationships, and more. Increased exposure—along with a humble posture of learning—can enhance our intercultural understanding and ability to effectively communicate the gospel across cultures (whether across the world or across the street).
- Jesus offers true healing to those struggling with drug and alcohol addiction, but deep, relational discipleship is often needed to help them continue walking in freedom for the long term.
- Sending recently recovered (and probably still recovering) addicts to the mission field puts both them and Christ's reputation at great risk. Sadly, this has shamed Christ many times. Whatever type of missionaries are sent, let them be rigorously selected, supported, and held accountable using biblical criteria.

Going Deeper: A Prince, the Bride, and Jesus

In this chapter, Lin reveals three problems keeping his people from Jesus that are true in many places across the Buddha Belt. These present a challenge and an opportunity for God's people everywhere.

- Many villages still have not received an intelligible gospel witness. No one has gone to tell them the good news of Jesus.
- Some Buddhists have heard an evangelistic message, but have been immunized against Jesus by the sinful behavior of grace-abusing Christians.
- Some Buddhists have heard an unclear gospel witness, because the messenger did not understand their worldview.

THA GYI'S STORY

Yangon City Lights

This chapter paints a picture of youth urbanization and opportunities for mission.

- Across the Buddha Belt, millions of young people are migrating to the city in search of a better life. Their need for jobs and relevant job skills presents diverse business and training opportunities for integrated mission endeavors.
- Young urban immigrants' openness to new ideas and desire to learn English present a unique opportunity for native English speakers who can teach.

New Friends, New Life

In this chapter Tha Gyi's friendship with two Christians begins a chain of events that eventually leads him to Jesus.

- Across the Buddha Belt, relationships with Christians are a key factor in many Buddhist people's journeys to Jesus. The urban youth's willingness to form friendships presents opportunities for both short- and long-term missions.

Something Missing

This chapter highlights Tha Gyi's cognitive dissonance between his new and old beliefs, confusion about his identity, and lost sense of belonging.

- Buddhist-background believers in Jesus often struggle to integrate their new faith, friends, and way of living with their previous lives. Deep and comprehensive discipleship is needed to help them work through areas of contradiction.
- To minimize confusion and frustration, Christians should carefully choose and explain key terms to Buddhists who are exploring Jesus, helping them understand how Christian and Buddhist worldviews relate.

Going Deeper: Repainting the White Colonialist Jesus

In this chapter, Tha Gyi shares some of the factors that have negatively affected the Burmese people's mental image of Jesus and how he believes this can be overcome.

- National history and ethnic identity have sadly tainted many people's views of Jesus in Myanmar and across the Buddha Belt. But deeply rooted, relational evangelism and discipleship can help these people see Jesus in more accurate and compelling ways. This is an invitation!

Appendix 3
How to Use Jesusinthebuddhabelt.com

This book is over, but God's redemptive work in the Buddha Belt—and the role you can play in it—continues! Our team has built a website to help facilitate that. Visit jesusinthebuddhabelt.com to:

- Sign up for free ongoing updates and resources that will help you keep learning, praying, and engaging with what God is doing among Buddhists and future publications
- Send feedback and ask questions
- Connect with our team and others doing mission in the Buddha Belt
- Access blog articles, curated images, and video-based content
- Download free prayer guides for the Buddha Belt
- Try some of our favorite recipes
- Join a prayer group
- Take a course to upgrade your knowledge and skills for mission
- Learn about short and long-term mission opportunities with our partnering organizations

Suggestions for Further Reading

Anderson, Courtney. *To the Golden Shore: The Life of Adoniram Judson.* Judson Press, 1988.

Cioccolanti, Steve. *From Buddha to Jesus: An Insider's View of Buddhism and Christianity.* Monarch Books, 2010.

Lim, David, Steve Spaulding, and Paul H. De Neui, editors. *Sharing Jesus in the Buddhist World.* William Carey Publishing, 2003.

Lim, David, and Paul H. De Neui, editors. *Communicating Christ in the Buddhist World.* William Carey Publishing, 2006.

Myint-U, Thant. *The River of Lost Footsteps: A Personal History of Burma.* Farrar, Straus and Giroux, 2008.

Shwe Wa, Maung. *Burma Baptist Chronicle.* Rangoon University Press, 1963.

Acknowledgments

Thank you to Vivian and the wonderful team at William Carey Publishing for taking a risk on an unknown author and for being a pleasure to work with.

Thank you, Nadi, for the love, patience, and skill you put into the wonderful illustrations in this book. You're amazing! (Contact Nadi at hninnadi.hna@gmail.com for inquiries.)

Thank you to the many wonderful family members, friends, colleagues, and mentors, without whose love, encouragement, and feedback this book would not exist. You know who you are.

Thank you, Greg, for your Christ-like example and instrumentality in my Myanmar journey. "Welcome to Burma!"

Thank you to my beautiful bride for supporting me in life and this book endeavor in more ways than anyone knows. I love you so so much.

visit us at missionbooks.org

Emerging Faith:
Lessons from Mission History in Asia

Paul H. de Neui, editor

No culture in the world is a blank slate; rather, we can look for the initiating, inviting work of the missio Dei already emerging from within every surprising source. This book showcases the writings of sixteen reflective practitioners who offer insights based on their study and experience of history. Highlighting key people and places, *Emerging Faith* surveys several Christian movements found in the mission history of Asia.

That Man Who Came to Us

Sawai Chinnawong (Author)
Paul H. De Neui (Author)

That Man Who Came to Us tells the story of the life of Jesus Christ through traditional Thai art. Artist Sawai Chinnawong employs the regions' popular distinctive artistic style originally used to depict Buddhist moral principles and other religious themes. A meditative and teaching tool, *That Man* is a simple yet powerful book that communicates Christ in both the Thai and English languages. The book also includes cultural notes and scripture references for further study.

www.ingramcontent.com/pod-product-compliance
Lightning Source LLC
Chambersburg PA
CBHW060602080526
44585CB00013B/657